# THE
# ENGLISH REVIEW

July, 1921.

EDITED BY
AUSTIN HARRISON

Published by Left of Brain Books

Copyright © 2021 Left of Brain Books

ISBN 978-1-396-32176-4

*First Edition*

# Table of Contents

# ODE TO PEACE

## By Lord Gorell

### I.

FAIR daughter of unconquerable Hope,
Who with the wistful blessing of a star
Piercest the ribbed and melancholy clouds
    That thy perpetual warders are,
    Stretch forth the pleading of thy hand,
From grief and loss the glutted weapons tear,
And let the constant passion of thy prayer
Breathe a new beauty through the wounded land,
Swell to new music on the troubled air.

### II.

Thou who wast nursed within the watery wastes
And ruined hearts of conflict, once again
The guns' uneasy silence greets thy birth,
    And thine inheritance is pain:
    A thousand hapless furies wail
About thy barque, and over the great sea
Still dimly lies safe harbourage for thee;
All mouthing to the gusts that yet prevail,
Waves lash the rocky coast-line enviously.

### III.

The world is like a soul that long has bowed
Its broken empire to Hell's gloomy might
And with an inward sickness turns at last
    Its wearied being towards the light;
    Timid it is; its power stands
In threadbare garments open to the scorn
Of devastating blasts, and half-forlorn

The high desires wring indecisive hands;
Night lingers on, distrustful of the morn.

IV.

Awake, awake! With angered resonance
The heavy tumult through the mind is rolled;
The dark mists shake about the ascending path
    And fitfully the prospect fold:
    Sweet Peace, be thou before our eyes
Guiding, earth's caravanners to the crest;
Storm-swept are the long ridges, and the quest
Even beyond the verge of vision lies,
Where tumult sinks and thy shy soul has rest.

V.

Night lingers on distrustful, but the day
Shall break upon our journey as we climb;
The peaks are flaming now, and presently,
    Led by the patient steps of Time,
    That shepherd of the human flocks,
Light shall descend with comfort richly hued,
Shall be a beacon for the multitude,
And new shall be the vision round the rocks
Of age-worn custom and internal feud.

VI.

Beyond, beyond, lie the deep realms of Hope
Bathed in thy presence, Peace; and there thy state
In starry benediction breathes out Love
    And dwells serene, dethroning Hate,
    The last and greatest victory:
Therein the shepherd, Time, himself shall stay
At rest beside his footsteps far away,
And all the motion of the earth shall be
The tranquil dawn of thine eternal day.

# NIGHT AND NOON: LYRICS

By John Helston

## NIGHT THROES.

In peaceful oceans of the dew,
　　The island juniper
Stand up and watch the night renew
　　Her starry hemisphere.

*"I'm in the berried hush, my love,*
　　*Where night is on the down.*
*I would the dews might rise above*
　　*My heart—and passion drown!"*

She heard the night wind leave the hill
　　A long dark league away...
A withered fen became her will,
　　Her womb a pit of clay.

## A CHURCHYARD.

Quaint pictures of the sun in power
And insurrections of the stone
The lichens dwelling on the tower
Have wrought for thrice a hundred years,
Where silently a sign appears—
A creeping shadow of the hour,
Appears, and then is gone.

Quietly as from the dial up yon
The clouds depose time's darkened ray,
Pale folk come in a cloud of thought—
The folk for whom time's ways are naught,
And with great eyes that answer none,
Pass me, and steal away.

# FLAMES

### By Dorothea Still


WHEN I am deep within your arms
My little, struggling flames expire;
The scorching of my restless life
Beneath your lips is quenched of fire.
Devouring points of trembling pride,
Anger's quick spark and smoking fear,
The blinding flash of sudden pain,
Die as they spring, and disappear
From memory.
                 The fiery tongues
Are still. Then is it death you hold
Upon your living breast—so numb,
So cold?
Held in your keeping lies a flame,
Flowering gold that does not dart
Nor spring
Up from the shelter of your heart.
The puny flickerings are dead:
But when I lie
Hid in this cavern of content,
Love and I
Rest quietly, for we are one
Red-warm, unwavering gleam, at peace:
And all tormented little fires
Must cease
Within the uncontending glow
—When on your heart so still I lie
You hold a flame—
And all my tortured burnings die.

# DESCENT: A MOSAIC

## By Hermon Ould


Come to me here on the summit of the hill, where God's breath frees from death and drives out fear. I greedily take my fill of creant life newborn, and take the universe to wife. Forlorn friend, intrigued by a sham Elysium, come!

Here on the slope, where the odour of the firs unlinks control and the coward soul—scared antelope—escapes the universe as 'twere a snare, I wait. Let me not seek you otherwhere, lest hate evict love by its shrill delirium. Come!

Lo! I am here, imprisoned in the town, where fecund life, seed of strife and nursed by fear, moves obscenely down to graceless death. Here I, inhaling death with every breath, will die, numb with the mystery of love, and dumb. Come!

# THE SPRING OF YESTERYEAR

## By Chris Massie

I PRAY thee seek to guide me, I am blind
    With frozen tears, and dark with every woe;
I hear no voices calling down the wind—
The breezes kiss me with a kiss unkind...
    My love is long-ago.

I am forgotten in long yesterday:
    My dreams are dead, my songs are all forgot.
The rustling grass I hear along the way
Is thousand-tongued with words that plead and pray...
    But what I was, is not.

The vital sunbeams flash and throb again,
    And April dawns embrace the dying stars;
There is a sweetest blessing in the rain,
But what I was has melted into pain...
    And I have many scars.

Alas! I feel the weight of human wrongs—
The murdered presence of remembered dead.
No sunny circumstance, no tender songs,
Can woo my heart from where my heart belongs
Or grant me what has fled.

The stars I see are calm in cruel peace,
    And April buds are cold in high disdain.
The nesting birds can feel their joys increase,
And love is deep as darkness in the trees...
    But I have loved in vain.

I am the hope that fled away in fear;
    I am the babe that never found a breast.
I have no thought, no vital feeling near—
I am the Spring—the Spring of Yesteryear—
    And now I look for rest.

# THISTLEDOWN

## By Horace Shipp

THE harsh wheels screech and turn, they wind
Unending cycles, till the mind
Is a hot road where lorries grind.

The buildings throb; the sunrays like hot rain
Beat down through senses to the shrivelled brain;
The houses blur behind a yellow stain.

Remote beyond sensation, passers-by
Pattern the pavement; their small shadows lie
More real than they beneath the hot, white sky.

Then sudden as the thought of beauty, frost
Amid Hell's flame tongues, aerial, eddying, lost
In light, gulfed in light, and airily tossed,

The thistledown from some far field is blown:
Live dust across the dead dust overgrown
With this fantastic foliage of stone,

This petrifaction where the passing feet
Will trample beauty rivelled in the heat.
Seed-time and harvest cease, but still the street

Blooms barren and the stone weeds never fail—
Stone barriers of the earth whereto the frail,
Pale silken argosies of seedlings sail.

And yet...and yet, the centuries creeping by,
The petrous petals of the town will lie
Scattered, its stone roots bare beneath the sky.

And in the summer silence, quietly grown,
Quietly like the thought of beauty, blown
Seeds of the thistle in the crevassed stone.

# SONG

## By Ethel Archer

### Aphrodite to Sappho.

Come, Love, awaken! O'er the wild salt sea,
Shadows strange-shapen whirl themselves and flee
As eddying mist, by storm winds overtaken,
And sunbeams kissed—the shafts all curled and shaken
In shuddering ecstasy!
Come, Love, nor list to tired dreams that twist
Thy lithe long limbs in fierce abandonment,
Awake, and learn of me the secret of the sea,
Whose meaning is the sum of all things blent
In fiercest harmony.

Soft winds are calling on the cloudy deep
(Like foam-flowers falling from the breasts of Sleep
Their Lotus-kiss is). Such a world forestalling
Of wanton blisses, that the fear of palling
Makes e'en the Sirens weep.
Ah me! What serpent hisses from out those
    purple 'bysses,
Far in the womb of the lone-lying sea.
She wakes! Nor dare he creep back to her soul, whence
    Sleep
Has torn aside the mist-hung drapery;
Too strange the way—and steep.

# AN OPEN LETTER TO THE REV. H. R. L. SHEPPARD

## By Filson Young

My Dear Dick,

Whenever I hear of you or think of you carrying on your gallant campaign at St. Martin's I feel a little angry; and I have been trying to discover why. You, of course, are devoted to the fatal course that can only end in martyrdom or an archbishopric, and your wonderful gifts are being expended, happily enough, I daresay; to give is to live, and to give oneself, expend oneself as completely as possible, is no doubt to live very completely. But I wonder what you really think of the channel through which your gift is flowing, and in which so much of it must be wasted. And I write this, not to involve you in controversy, for which you have neither time nor (thank Heaven) taste, but rather to attempt to discover why many of the people who sympathise with you most keenly, and would like to help so gallant a fighter, feel the uselessness of throwing time or energy into a quicksand.

Everyone who thinks at all is agreed that the centres of influence of human society are not in a very healthy condition. And complex as are the results of this condition they are really traceable to one main cause—the surprising outbreak of panic selfishness that has followed upon the great war. The rarest virtue at present, in public or in private life, is that by which men and women forgo advantages to themselves in the interests of the majority of their fellows. The worst of it is that selfishness defeats itself. If happiness were really attainable through the doctrine of everyone for himself, the world would at once become a very happy place. The whole experience of mankind has proved this method to be a dead failure, and when everyone is bent singly on his own benefit, everyone is more or less unhappy. The religion of Christianity is the greatest of all organised attempts to cure this devastating plague of selfishness.

There have been times in which it has been surprisingly successful; and it is worth while to consider the extent to which it is succeeding at this moment. The voices of the bells still summon us daily to repentance, praise, and prayer; with daily less and less response to their invitation. The tongues of men sound louder and ever louder; their sound, with its gospel of cheap expediency multiplied and resonated by every device of science, is gone out into all lands, and their words to the world's end. But the tongues of angels are almost silent; poetry, intellect, art, are at a discount. Now the Christian religion has the advantage of an immense organisation ready made. In England, for example, a vast number of persons are specifically educated and endowed in order that they may lead the Christian life and spread its benefits to others. And the first thing we find is a general outcry on the part of parsons and other endowed persons that their endowment is too low; that it cannot be done on the money, in other words. And this while the income of the Church, if it were pooled, would be amply sufficient to maintain its ministers. Here is the first great departure from the teaching of Jesus, who knew very well that teachers of a spiritual gospel must live very simple lives if they are to be listened to. A large income does not make a good man better, provided he is free to live poor, as the clergy are. If it did, the cathedral closes of places like Wells and Lichfield would be great centres of spiritual and Christian force; but they are not. The Church, to put it bluntly, is not in it with the cinema as an active and determining element in the lives of the people of England.

We all know men who really believe and preach the ideal of Jesus and try to live it. But how many of them succeed, and on what lines do they try? For that is the root of the matter, and I am quite sure that the reason that the Church is so pitiable a failure in England to-day is that its officers have drifted so very far from the ideals of the master they profess to serve. If Jesus were vicar of a large London parish church to-day, what would he do? Of one thing we may be very sure; his life would be a simple one. The life of the modern priest in such a situation is immensely complicated. Telephones, secretaries, guilds, lists of hourly appointments filled up weeks ahead, dinner parties (not many of these), dragoonings of workers in complex organisations—these are not easily compatible with the saint-like life. I think that we should find that the vicar who came nearest to his ideal would reduce his organisations and complexities to a minimum and be found many hours of every day in his church, to be consulted and talked to and, if necessary, argued with—not mouth to ear as in a confessional, but publicly and casually, and for the benefit of all.

This note of simplicity is one of the hardest things to achieve in the modern world, but without it there can be no real power or greatness. I know several saints; but whatever their worldly circumstances they all live remarkably simple lives, and they always have time for other people. Even the great deities of the business world know this secret. Great business men like Lord Northcliffe or Lord Leverhulme live extremely simple lives—that is to say, everything is eliminated that does not bear on the main purpose. They go without many things that go to make life pleasant for the ordinary man— above all, they forgo that casual intercourse with their fellow-men which is at once the greatest absorber of time, and one of the best ways of spending it. Men need not emulate them whose lives are not dedicated to any particular purposes; and (fortunately for the sanity of the race) most of us are neither trying very hard to make, nor are bound to the wheel of, a fortune. The average Christian priest is bound to a very definite purpose, yet I venture to say that he has not half the self-dedication of a Selfridge or a Dunhill.

"Oh," says the parson, "but Jesus lived in simple times, and I live in very complex ones; if he lived in the world now he would mix with it, partake of its activities, etc., etc." Yes, but with what part of it? Man stands in all ages in the same relationship to eternal facts and truths. The Pharisees based the traps they set for Jesus on this old humbugging fallacy, and were promptly bowled out—one would have thought for all time. People are really surprising. The up-to-date parson thinks it right to mingle with all sides of life, and what with dining out, Bible classes, dancing, sacraments, politics, cultivating the rich giver and superintending the poor receiver, must get into a dreadful muddle. He quotes the wedding feast, the Publican, the Magdalene. As to these, if the modern parson, and what he ought to stand for, were the real centre of interest of every dinner party as Jesus was of his one rather casual wedding feast (when the wine was forgotten!) there would be something to be said for him; but the dining-out parson knows very well that if he spoke like Jesus he would not be asked again. The Publicans of the Bible were merely people of an unpopular social class; and if the parson showed a preference for the table of an undertaker to that of a duke, or of a pawnbroker to that of a Secretary of State, he might claim to be following the great example. But he does not. As for Magdalenes, they are the most attractive and forgivable of all sinners, the pets of reformers of all ages, and Jesus only showed his humanity in his understanding and sympathy with them.

Someone may say, "Why attack the poor parson? He is doing his best, and if you do not like his ministrations you are not obliged to endure them." But is he doing his best? Or has he become enmeshed in the folds of a moribund organisation which makes anything like his best impossible? You, at any rate, realise what an immense amount of time, energy and money is being absorbed by this great curative business of religion, which in fact is only an anodyne, and is not curing anything at all. Many men are complacent and indulgent to the Churches because they have stood in the past for things noble and sublime, and have fought in the van of brave causes. But this complacency and indulgence may be seriously overdone. A church, like a state, cannot live for ever on its past. A rotting corpse is not beautiful, even though it once was animated by a noble spirit; it is a part of death, and must be put away so that life shall take its place. That is the law, eternal and inexorable. I do not say that the Church is a rotting corpse; but there are some unmistakable signs of mortification that begin to offend the nostrils of humanity, and suggest that a rigorous amputation and chopping off must be resorted to if such healthy life as remains is to be saved and made useful to mankind.

The Church, following its usual practice of helping those who have already helped themselves, is now beginning to kow-tow to Labour. When Labour was the under dog it got little countenance from the Church; but now when every vested interest is trembling before it the Church discovers in it a great power for good. Maybe; but the people who want help now, and among whom there is far more real suffering in these bad times than among the wage-earners, are the middle, educated classes. They have been the real support of the Church, which is the only kind of organisation which might be said to represent them. What is the Church doing to protect them from the organised tyranny and greed of the shopkeeper, the skilled artisan, the provision-dealer, the owner of house-property—from everyone, in fact, who has got any kind of a stranglehold on the daily life of the community? Very little, I am afraid. In toadying to Labour, which has never needed it and intends to proceed without it, the advanced party in the Church is committing one of the most humiliating acts of its career.

And what, I wonder, do you think of belonging to the organisation, vowed to the gospel of Nazareth, which has just spent thousands of pounds on proving before the Lord Chancellor and several Bishops the momentary misconduct of a priest whose guilt, if guilt it was, was in direct exception and contradiction to the whole tenor of his life? What of a Church that makes of such an incident an unsavoury scandal that feeds the appetites of the nasty-minded for months, and will fill old ladies, listening to their favourite Lenten adviser, with dreadful misgivings and improper speculations? If you, my dear Dick, had been Bishop of Lincoln, you would have said: "Your wife does not believe this; neither need I. If you are guilty, tell me, and I will help to kill this scandal and save you from any possible repetition of it; if you are innocent, tell me, and I will believe you." But you were not Bishop of Lincoln; and as a result a most unsavoury incense has gone up. If you had heard the silly kind of comment that went on in clubs and other places where the clergy do not go you would realise the harm done, and the hindrance to people like yourself, and all you stand for, by the dull worldliness and stupid insincerity of what may be called the official Church.

But perhaps you do realise it. What are you and men like you (if there are any) going to do about it? It seems to me that there is one way in which you might unite, and give a lead to, all the moral and intellectual forces which ought to be, and are not, our guide in England to-day—and that is by helping people to see that this is no moment for destruction. It is notoriously easier to destroy than to build; to-day everyone seems to want to destroy, and no one to build. And at a time when there is nothing like agreement as to what it is we want to build on the cleared ground, the folly of pulling down ought to be doubly apparent. If we can check the craze for destroying all our imperfect institutions we may tide over a bad time, and come to something like an understanding of what it is we really want. There is a lesson for the Church to teach, if it is still really a teaching institution. But is it?

Yours without repentance,

Filson Young.

# LORD MILNER'S MEMORANDUM ON THE EVENTS OF MARCH, 1918

## By Walter Shaw Sparrow

### *Author of "The Fifth Army in March, 1918"*

MANY persons wish to know for what reason Lord Milner singled out *The New Statesman*, a weekly review, when he decided that he would publish, in a crude and uncorrected form, a selected Memorandum from the secret history of March, 1918. By this act he has revived officially grave charges against Sir Hubert Gough and the Fifth Army which there was reason to hope had been laid to rest for ever by detailed evidence supported by convincing proof. Lord Milner cannot have supposed that his indiscretion would attract little attention.

He cannot regard the document as his private property, for it relates how he, when head of the War Office, went over to France on a very urgent mission, in order that he might report to the Cabinet personally on the position of affairs there. Two British armies were retreating on French soil; opinion in France was feverish and embittered; slander brought charges of cowardice against our officers and men; and the Cabinet in London was face to face with the fact that it had refused to supply Haig with enough men and guns. What Lord Milner did in France, then, must be a story that belongs to the nation; so it should have been sent on the same day to the nation's Press. But no Minister of 1918 is at all eager that the searchlight of truth should play freely over and into the Cabinet's failure—a failure as harmful to certain military and naval advisers as it is to the Prime Minister and his lay colleagues. Naval advisers must be included, for it is reasonable to believe that vast numbers of British troops were not detained in the British Isles without some advice from the Admiralty. While our Eastern coast was profusely manned for intrepid defence against chimeras, Haig was expected to achieve safety by gambling with enormous risks. His front had been increased to 125 miles; his divisions had been weakened by the loss of three battalions apiece; and although he had in all only 58 divisions of infantry, with only 10 battalions in each, his ranks had not been filled up by drafts. Scarcely a unit in his armies had its full complement of men. These facts cannot have been unknown to Lord Milner, unless Ministers find it convenient in a time of crisis never to focus any fact by which a Cabinet and its advisers have undermined their utility.

If his mission to France had been arranged properly, a very different memorandum would have been written. Our troops had fought through four days and three nights when Lord Milner arrived at Boulogne at 6.30 on Sunday evening, March 24th; and the useful and necessary thing was to hold a conference before midnight at the main centre of the battle's facts—Gough's headquarters. "The great mystery," says Milner himself, "was the breakdown of the Fifth Army, which so far was not explained." And a conference at Gough's headquarters could have been easily ordered before Milner left London. If Haig and Pétain and Byng had been present, the whole truth would have been known, and then discussed, in all its plainness, and Milner's mission would have been rational.

But reasonableness was either fast asleep or only half-awake. Though Milner, with youthful energy, motored a prodigious number of miles in two days, sometimes at 40 miles an hour, he kept far away from Gough's headquarters, and gleaned what he could get elsewhere, at Montreuil and Versailles, at Paris and Compiègne, and also at Doullens. General Wilson, too, was motoring in France, also without visiting the Fifth Army though his presence in England as a motorist would have heartened the youthful reinforcements who had been detained at home far too long. Note, too, that Gough was not summoned to any of the conferences attended by Milner. He was not present at Compiègne on the 25th, and next day he was absent from the great meeting at Doullens, which was attended by Byng, Horne, and Plumer. In plain words, though Lord Milner was sent out to investigate on the spot what had actually happened as the result of Ludendorff's offensive, nothing was done to get first-hand knowledge from the Fifth Army.

Though Milner did not visit the Fifth Army, he was obliged to pass judgment on it, and I am not at all surprised that his verdict was based on grievous errors. I have known for a long time that G.H.Q. gathered many misleading notions from several sources, as from the incessant reports, often delayed, that came by day and night from so many miles of moving front. Also I have known that G.H.Q. visited Gough only once during the battle. For the tragical need of men pressed more and more on Haig and his staff; how to bring up and use reinforcements without endangering the Channel ports was a tremendous anxiety; and G.H.Q. must have been terribly surprised and frightened by the dangers which its own dispositions had invited. It had overburdened a third portion of the entire British front with all the risks, partly because the other two-thirds drew nearer and nearer to the Channel ports, leaving less and less room for a retreat; and partly because Haig believed that the heaviest German attack would fall north-west of Flesquières salient, between Sensée river and the Bapaume-Cambrai road. Ludendorff had learnt that Gough's front of 42 miles was the weakest portion; so he assembled against it an enormous force which he regarded as irresistible, and which comprised 43 well-manned divisions, besides powerful reinforcements. Gough began the battle with 11 divisions in line, one division in reserve, and sufficient cavalry to equal another foot division in man-power. Two reserve divisions were withheld from the front by G.H.Q.; one came up on the evening of March 21st, and the other arrived early next day. Only one British reinforcement remained under Gough: it was the 8th Division. Another reinforcement, our 35th Division, passed with Gough's northern corps on to Byng's territory, during the night of March 25th-26th, because of grave mishaps in the Third Army.

These mishaps were very active when Milner arrived at Boulogne and motored at once to G.H.Q. at Montreuil. Yet he makes no reference to them. During the day Byng's centre had been broken between 4th Corps and 5th Corps, and his right wing had given way along the line Combles-Morval-Lesbœufs, despite the most gallant efforts of Gough's left wing north of its boundary. Gaps also had formed between the divisions of 5th Corps, with the result that they had to close up north-westward, and thus away from Gough. In the evening of March 24th, when Milner, after visiting G.H.Q., began his long motor journey to Versailles (as though Gough and his headquarters had no value at all), the Third Army was out of touch with the Fifth, though the Fifth's troops at Longueval were holding Byng's ground. From Longueval Gough's line ran down to Ham-sur-Somme; then behind the river to Péronne, and on to Brie and a point north-west of Flavy, where a German salient west of the river began. This salient ran south-east a little west of Morchain, a little east of Mesnil, down to the Libermont lines, and then to the east of Guiscard and the west of Chauny. During the day three French divisions had come up without guns, and with no more small-arm ammunition than their men carried. Two gunless French divisions had arrived on the previous day, March 23rd, and another sent units into the fight on the 25th; but, of course, being very ill-equipped, they could not do justice to their fine qualities. By the evening of the 27th ten French divisions had counterbalanced the huge reinforcements which the Germans south of the Somme were adding to their immense odds. When we remember that the French for a long time were badly equipped, it is not surprising that the German penetration by the end of the seventh day was deepest where the French were most numerous—in the Montdidier sector. This means that the only organised power south of the Somme was Gough's force. Milner could not have motored here and there, always in safety, if the Fifth Army's condition had been as crippled and ineffectual as he believed.

Milner was told on his arrival at Boulogne not only that Gough's Army was shattered, but also that a breach was effected between Byng's forces and the French. There was a gap between Byng's right at Bazentin and Gough's left at Longueval, no doubt; but from the Longueval sector there were no French troops for a crow-flight of 22 miles. On the evening of March 24th the French troops nearest to Longueval were some elements of the 22nd Division near Hombleux, with our 30th Division south of them. From Longueval down to these French troops, who had British units among them, France was defended by the Fifth Army; so it is fantastic to say that a breach had been made between Byng and the French.

Wherever Milner went he was never asked either to visit Gough or to correct the false impressions which he had gained from distant and inaccurate information. And he says: "It was clearly useless to speculate with our present knowledge about the causes or the exact course of events in this quarter, but the effect of what had happened on the general situation was, of course, perfectly clear, and did not need to be dwelt upon." Amazing! "Speculation" certainly would have been useless, but a personal interview with the leader of our Fifth Army would have cleared up many dangerous misunderstandings. If Milner had published a correct map giving the battle positions during his visit to France, with the divisions in line and reserve, both British and French, his readers would see that he learnt little that was accurate about the Fifth and Third Armies.

Even Pétain, on March 25th, told Milner that the Fifth Army, as an army, had ceased to exist; that it would have to be completely reorganised; and also that it had now been placed under his (Pétain's) orders. As it had taken Pétain five whole days to bring up six ill-equipped divisions, that retreated more rapidly than Gough's, the need of organised reinforcements was really the main point to be discussed; but Pétain did his best in a very difficult situation, and it was he, not Foch, who contributed to the saving of Amiens. Propaganda says that "Foch moved up the French troops which, by a margin of hours, saved Amiens." Nothing could be more false. Milner proves that Pétain after listening to criticism was willing to raise his maximum reinforcements from 15 to 24 divisions; and those that helped to save Amiens were the first ten. But the main factors of all were British tenacity against amazing odds, and our airmen's bombing of the German reserves and reinforcements, united to the fact that a widespread and long advance over devastated land and broken roads and bridges had become its own worst foe, just as Foch's became in the autumn of 1918.

And now let us draw closer to the complete falsity of the information that Milner picked up at Montreuil, Versailles, and Compiègne. The Committee at Versailles had been ineffectual, and its members were very sore indeed, as we learn from Peter Wright. Haig and Pétain were regarded as conspirators, and Foch was very tired of being an adviser with no power. He wanted to rise into some sort of Supreme Command; but the French Pétainites were about as numerous as the French Fochites. What Foch needed was enough British support apart from that at Versailles, and he found it in Milner and Wilson, who represented the British Cabinet. Milner's Memorandum is mainly—not a cool and searchingly impartial inquiry into what he calls "the course of events" along the fighting fronts, but—an account of the steps by which Foch was lifted into Supreme Command, not without a general misunderstanding of Pétain's great gifts. Pétain was too unemotional to be rated then at his just value. He was always exceedingly cool and self-possessed, and never in word or expression betrayed his real feelings. Further, as the whole drama was one of bringing up reinforcements from distant places, and as Pétain would not promise that they could be brought up more swiftly than he deemed possible, his speech at Doullens seemed too cold and too cautious. Milner says, indeed: "None of his listeners seemed very happy or convinced. Wilson and Haig evidently were not; indeed, Wilson made an interjection which almost amounted to a protest. Foch, who had been so eloquent the day before (March 25th), said not a word. But, looking at his face—he sat opposite me—I could see that he was still dissatisfied, very impatient, and evidently thinking that things could and must be done more quickly." It was Foch's fervour, his imperious emotionalism, that impressed the Doullens Conference, and both Haig and Pétain were relieved, for both were convinced that advice from a Committee was the negation of military good sense, and both had suffered too much from such fussy and far-travelling motorists as would have been intolerable to Marlborough and Wellington. Foch was too autocratic to bear interference; but in a few days, and through three months, he needed and received the most strenuous support from his British friends, for he began his reign with three defeats, and one of them was exceedingly humiliating.

Now, as everyone was thinking in March of urging up reinforcements, rumours and misconceptions gained far too much influence. Among the misconceptions was the belief that Byng's troops were martyrs, that "they had been let down badly by Gough's men, who were mishandled." Troops in the field very often imagine that when they are obliged to fall back they have been let down by their neighbours; and it happened that Byng's right adopted this common error, and sent it on to Byng, who accepted it as a fact. Thence it passed to G.H.Q., and to Milner, Wilson, Foch, Rawlinson, Pétain, Paris, London, the House of Commons, and endless public slander. Foch was so misinformed about the Fifth Army that one of his early acts as generalissimo was to speak with cutting rudeness to Gough, who met the affront as a British Officer should, with cool and quiet dignity.

Milner, too, was unjust to Gough. In his Memorandum there is no mention of Gough's name, and he adulates Byng. Byng was at the Doullens Conference, unlike Gough, and Milner says of him: "I was especially struck by the attitude of General Byng, who, commanding the Third Army, had had to bear the greatest and indeed an almost unendurable strain." This proves that Milner knew nothing about the Third Army, which from the first day was well-manned for modernised defence. On a narrow front of $26\frac{2}{3}$ miles there were 17 divisions, and the Germans had 24; while Gough on a much wider front had a much smaller force, and the power that assailed him had 43 divisions. If Byng's strain was almost unendurable, it was not because he fought against great odds. Reinforcements came to him from many quarters. On March 26th, for instance, about six miles of his right were held by Fifth Army men; and early in the afternoon, when the Conference at Doullens began, Australian and New Zealand reinforcements, hurrying into action, closed two gaps by which the northern Ancre line was outflanked, and through which the foe had advanced as far as Colincamps.

Though Milner learnt little about the battle's facts, his Memorandum will be for all time very valuable as history, for it proves that neither Haig's G.H.Q. nor Pétain's G.Q.G. had either correct information or control; and it shows clearly, in its repetition of inaccurate conjectures and beliefs, how slanderous rumours about the Fifth Army originated, and won belief even in high quarters.

# THE NAIL.
## A Story of the Old Régime

## By George A. Scott

"The horrors of justice under the Old Régime are notorious," remarked the clever lawyer, as we sat in his cell one night in Moscow Gaol, drinking hot tasteless coffee. We'll call it coffee by courtesy. As a matter of fact it was coloured water—coloured with the remains of some coffee grounds, which had been boiled over and over again to help keep up the deception that we were really drinking coffee. The other cells were asleep. Silence reigned throughout the entire iron town. The ceaseless ticking of the great prison clock only helped to intensify it.

> "The dull day is dead and the darkness is near,
> Through the bars, the purple rays peep;
> And hushed are the sobbings of sorrowful prayer,
> Silence reigns; the cells are asleep—"

Some prisoner had scribbled the verse on the white-washed wall of the cell, and the young Russian-speaking officer could not help thinking as he read it that it filled the prevailing atmosphere with a terrible sense of realism. However, he poured himself out another mug of steaming liquid, settled himself on the iron bedstead with his knees tucked under his chin, and made ready to listen to the lawyer's story.

"Ah," continued the lawyer, "we prisoners live in comparative paradise. The worst they can do to us is to shoot us. In the old days that bed which you are sitting on was locked to the wall all day, and if the occupant of the cell did not behave himself it was kept locked to the wall all night."

His visitor examined the bed closely. It was a curious bed. A sort of iron basket arrangement, attached to the wall by two hinges. In the old days it lifted up and locked itself on to a notched bar, with a musical click. When let down by the warder in the evening, it developed a leg, and thus was supported by the two hinges on the wall side and the adjustable leg on the outer side. As the Bolshevist authorities had lost all the keys of these beds, and were unable to make new ones, the locks had all been broken; so that the beds could be used both day and night by the inhabitants of a cell.

The young officer was all attention. He knew that the lawyer's opening remark heralded a good story. And a good story could do much to while away the monotony of a tedious night, or day—there being really very little difference between the two, for it was in any case but a sorry apology for a sun that rose late and set early.

"Yes," went on the lawyer. "Prisoners were treated in a vastly different manner after the fatal attempt to overthrow the Government, in 1905. But let me relate you the case I have in mind."

He was just about to begin his narrative when the cell door opened softly. A friendly guard appeared. The prison guard was changed every week. Some weeks the prisoners were lucky in their guards; other weeks, less so. This was a lucky week. The guard in the corridor of the particular row of cells which the lawyer and the British prisoners occupied, happened to be, as so many Soviet guards and soldiers are, a Bolshevist, not from conviction so much as from the means it offered him to support his wife and family. Such guards were invariably kind and humane towards the prisoners, so long as there was no higher authority about, in the shape of a member of the Extraordinary Commission. They invariably unlocked the doors at night and allowed prisoners to visit each other. The lawyer gave the guard a piece of black bread, which was more welcome to him than the sight of a bag full of gold would have been. The guard left the cell, to keep "cave," and one by one a number of other prisoners quietly entered. They always congregated in the little lawyer's cell, as he was by far the most interesting and entertaining personality in the whole prison.

He settled them as comfortably as he could and boiled up his coffee again on a cleverly improvised little stove, fashioned out of an old biscuit-tin, which he fed with paper. It was a long process, and the cell was filled with smoke, so that he was obliged to open the barred window for a time.

At last all were served, sitting on the straw-mattress, sipping their so-called coffee and munching the crusts of black bread which they had brought with them. This, then, is the story they listened to, retold in the lawyer's own words:

It was in 1907, in this very cell, that I first came across Dmitri Gavrilov. He was an ardent revolutionary, and one of the most noble creatures it has ever been my lot to know. In those days my legal calling often took me to the prison, for, a lover of freedom myself, I always did all in my power to aid political offenders, who were then, as now, in so many cases the victims of an unjust tyranny. For the spirit of a true, honest and patriotic revolutionary can no more be broken than can the will of a true, honest and patriotic royalist. I do not speak of anarchists and other extremists, since they, as we already know, have proved themselves in no way lesser tyrants than were the minions of the Old Régime; they merely kill by a quicker process. In this alone they are more humane. Yes, only Death has power to stem the torrent of divine utterances which fall from the lips of honest men, whatever their politics. No life sacrificed for an ideal is lived in vain; yet, I trow, alas! that many who gave their lives to bring about the Russian Revolution now sleep restlessly in their graves. But that is the natural tragedy of all great sacrifices. Long chaotic periods must pass before martyrs are honoured in the progressive scheme of humanity. Christ died on the Cross nearly two thousand years ago; and it is sometimes difficult to realise that He did not die in vain.

Dmitri Gavrilov had been languishing in gaol since 1905. Following that sorry and ineffective bid for freedom, the Government had had so many people to punish, that two years had elapsed before his case was inquired into. As a result of the enquiry he was committed for trial on a charge of treason and sedition, and was allowed to engage a lawyer to conduct his defence. He did not propose to put up any defence, but an admirer of his called on me, and gave me the full details of the case. I forthwith decided to visit Gavrilov in prison and to offer him my services. I arrived at the prison, where, on explaining my business, I was immediately conducted to the cell—this very cell—occupied by Gavrilov. As I had figured rather prominently in many political cases at various times he knew me well by name, and received me with a dignified courtesy.

"It is good of you to come, my friend," he said, "but I fear that your kindly errand must prove vain. I was arrested on suspicion. There are no facts against me. Nevertheless, in spite of anything you may say in my defence, I am fore-doomed. Did I for a moment think I could escape, I should lie as cleverly as I have often done in the past, in order that I might carry on the good work. But since 1905, such prevarications cannot help me. The authorities look upon me as a dangerous person, and at best I shall be sentenced to exile in Siberia—a living death. I love Russia, and as a patriot I can only recognise a revolutionary court. There exists no other court in this country which has the right to try me for treason."

Like King Charles of England, he considered that he could only be tried by his equals. In vain I expostulated with him.

"My friend," I cried, "let me try to gain you your liberty. I have saved many." But he only repeated his last statement. I argued long with him and eventually, seeing my evident distress, he consented to let me conduct the case for his defence. I then left him. Outside, at the gate, I was insultingly stopped by a gendarme officer. His overbearing attitude annoyed me. At that moment he seemed to me to be incarnate of all the injustices of the system. I was in any case overwrought after my conversation with Gavrilov, whose proud, dignified and calm demeanour had impressed me profoundly. The man was a minor god—perhaps unnecessarily quixotic—but a man of high principle nevertheless, who had the courage of his convictions—convictions which to me seemed perfectly reasonable and inspiring. In a fit of temper I struck the officer with all my force, knocked his hat off, and, as he was about to draw his sword on me, seized that weapon and gave him a thorough beating with it. He bellowed like a bull for assistance. Quite a number of people had witnessed his discomfiture. A policeman rushed up to arrest me. But the officer had recognised me. I was a well-known character, even in those days. Without another word he ordered his men to disperse the crowd. He knew that my arrest, in the circumstances, would give rise to a storm of ridicule in social circles, at his expense. For he was quite twice my size, and I had relieved him of his sword—the greatest indignity a Russian officer could suffer, at that time. He would become a laughing-stock, the public merriment only being accentuated by the fact of my arrest. So he turned on his heel and walked away.

The incident, however, reached the ears of his chief, who knew and respected me well, although we always quarrelled over politics. I was looked upon as somewhat of an eccentric; for parting with his sword, the subject of my encounter was eventually forced to resign. This goes to prove that an officer of the gendarmerie of Old Russia was not on all occasions a God Almighty.

I did not see my client until the following week—in court. In spite of his two years of acute physical suffering in this cell, which in those days was infinitely less comfortable than I have made it, he was as firm and upright as ever—a very eagle of a man. His case was duly presented. I argued, pleaded, expostulated, laughed and wept, making others to laugh and weep by virtue of my skill as an orator. I held the court. Never before had I made such a speech. I surpassed myself and delighted and moved my listeners.

I was just about to finish the most brilliant defence I had ever made in my life when the accused interrupted my flow of words. Quite calmly, he thanked me for my efforts on his behalf.

"You are wasting much beauty of language and much energy, my kind friend," he said. "Forgive me for having put you to so much trouble. Light has come to me. Alone by my presence here I am being false to my self-imposed principles."

He then faced the court, and proceeded to tell them that, according to their standards, he was guilty of treason, sedition and conspiracy—that he had deliberately plotted the overthrow of Tsardom—yet, in spite of this, that they had no right to judge him. They were dirt in his eyes. A court consisting of such vermin had no right to exist. He hated them; spat on them...

A few weeks later he was sentenced...to death. Charges brought by himself against himself (to screen other more violent revolutionaries), implicating him in the assassination of two unpopular governors, were taken as sufficient evidence of guilt.

The day before his execution was to have taken place I again visited him in prison, this time to bid him good-bye. The man's indomitable spirit had roused in me the highest possible feelings of admiration. I was greatly grieved that he should have brought matters to such a pass through his quixotic behaviour. I shall never forget his parting words to me—words which the prison authorities overheard:

"How can a snake kill a God? How can a Devil slay a Deity? Oh, yes! I shall die all right; but *they* won't kill me! Do you think for a minute that I shall let *their* foul minions rob *me* of God's good gift of life? I myself shall render unto God that which He of His bounty bestowed."

I never saw him again. He was conducted to a condemned cell. Once there, he was divested of every stitch of clothing; and from the cell was taken everything which could possibly have been used by him for the purpose of self-destruction. I said "everything." I should have added the word "almost."

An old kettle-lid had wedged itself in between the wall and the iron bedstead, and had escaped detection; likewise—a nail. But this nail was concealed in a vastly different manner than was the kettle-lid. The prisoner had buried it in the flesh of his leg, and the authorities had ignored the wound. For, was not the man about to die? And what need had a condemned man of a doctor, to dress a small wound in the leg?

The flap of the cell door remained open that night, and an armed guard watched the prisoner through the opening, lest the latter should himself, by some criminal act, rob the gallows of its prey.

The prisoner was to die at 5 a.m. About 2 a.m. he was seized with a terrible fit of convulsions. The guard, fearful that he should die from natural causes, sent for the prison doctor, who, after examining the condemned man, diagnosed the case as one of acute malaria. He gave orders that the naked prisoner on the iron bedstead should have a heavy rug thrown over his quivering limbs. This was exactly what the prisoner wanted. So far, so good. The convulsions under the coarse covering continued before the eyes of the startled superstitious watcher. They became mightier and mightier and were no longer simulated. The guard again summoned the prison doctor, who snatched the covering from off the dead man. It had taken him a long time to die, and he had uttered no cry of pain. The hot blood gushed from the severed artery in his throat, where the jagged edge of the old rusty kettle-lid had done its work, slowly, but effectively; and the long nail was firmly embedded in the heart of the prisoner. Concealed by the coarse rug, he had drawn it from his leg, and had lain on it, forcibly, deliberately...

The lawyer stopped talking, as the door opened, and the excited guard looked in:

"Quick, back to your cells! A car has arrived in the yard. An inspection is imminent."

Swiftly and quietly, the visitors stole back to their respective cells. The doors closed in a series of little metallic clicks. The lawyer was alone. Silence reigned. The cells were asleep.

# THE POMPILI[1]

## By Henri Fabre

THE victims of many Wasps that hunt prey on behalf of their larvæ allow themselves to be operated upon by the paralyser, submitting stupidly, without offering much resistance. The mandibles gape, the legs kick and protest, the body wriggles and twists; and that is all. They have no weapons capable of contending with the assassin's dagger. I should like to see the huntress grappling with an imposing adversary, one as crafty as herself, an expert layer of ambushes and, like her, bearing a poisoned dirk. I should like to see the bandit armed with the stiletto confronted with another bandit equally familiar with the use of that weapon. Is such a duel possible? Yes, it is quite possible and even common. On the one side are the Pompili, the champions who are always victorious; on the other hand are the Spiders, the champions who are always overthrown.

Who that has diverted himself, however little, with the study of insects does not know the Pompili? Against old walls, at the foot of the banks beside unfrequented footpaths, in the stubble after the harvest, in the tangles of dry grass, wherever the Spider spreads her nets, who has not seen them busily at work, now running hither and thither, at random, their wings raised and quivering above their backs, now moving from place to place in flights long or short? They are hunting for a quarry which might easily turn the tables and itself prey upon the trapper lying in wait for it.

The Pompili feed their larvæ solely on Spiders; and the Spiders feed on any insect commensurate with their size that is caught in their nets. While the first possess a sting, the second have two poisoned fangs. Often their strength is equally matched; indeed, the advantage is not seldom on the Spider's side. The Wasp has her ruses of war, her cunningly premeditated strokes; the Spider has her wiles and her set traps; the first has the advantage of great rapidity of movement, while the second is able to rely upon her perfidious web; the one has a sting which contrives to penetrate the exact point to cause paralysis, the

---

[1] Translated by Alexander Teixeira de Mattos. Copyright U.S.A., 1921, by Dodd, Mead & Co., Inc. All rights reserved.

other has fangs which bite the back of the neck and deal sudden death. We find the paralyser on the one hand and the slaughterer on the other. Which of the two will become the other's prey?

If we consider only the relative strength of the adversaries, the power of their weapons, the virulence of their poisons and their different modes of action, the scale would very often be weighted in favour of the Spider. Since the Pompilus always emerges victorious from this contest, which appears to be full of peril for her, she must have a special method, of which I would fain learn the secret.

In our part of the country, the most powerful and courageous Spider-huntress is the Ringed Pompilus, clad in black and yellow. She stands high on her legs; and her wings have black tips, the rest being yellow, as though exposed to smoke, like a bloater. Her size is about that of the Hornet. She is rare. I see three or four of her in the course of the year; and I never fail to halt in the presence of the proud creature, rapidly striding through the dust of the fields when the dog-days arrive. Its audacious air, its uncouth gait, its war-like bearing long made me suspect that to obtain its prey it had to make some impossible, terrible, unspeakable capture. And my guess was correct. By dint of waiting and watching I beheld that victim; I saw it in the huntress' mandibles. It is the Black-bellied Tarantula, the terrible Spider who slays a Carpenter-bee or a Bumble-bee outright with one stroke of her weapon; the Spider who kills a Sparrow or a Mole; the formidable creature whose bite would perhaps not be without danger to ourselves. Yes, this is the bill of fare which the proud Pompilus provides for her larva.

This spectacle, one of the most striking with which the Hunting Wasps have ever provided me, has as yet been offered to my eyes but once. I can still see the intrepid poacher dragging by the leg, at the foot of the wall, the monstrous prize which she had just secured, doubtless at no great distance. At the base of the wall was a hole, an accidental chink between some of the stones. The Wasp inspected the cavern, not for the first time: she had already reconnoitred it and the premises had satisfied her. The prey, deprived of the power of movement, was waiting somewhere, I know not where; and the huntress had gone back to fetch it and store it away. It was at this moment that I met her. The Pompilus gave a last glance at the cave, removed a few small fragments of loose mortar; and with that her preparations were completed.

The Tarantula was introduced, dragged along, belly upwards, by one leg. I did not interfere. Presently the Wasp reappeared on the surface and carelessly pushed in front of the hole the bits of mortar which she had just extracted from it. Then she flew away. It was all over. The egg was laid; the insect had finished for better or for worse; and I was able to proceed with my examination of the burrow and its contents.

The Pompilus has done no digging. It is really an accidental hole with spacious winding passages, the result of the mason's negligence and not of the Wasp's industry. The closing of the cavity is quite rough and ready. A few crumbs of mortar, heaped up before the doorway, form a barricade rather than a door. A mighty hunter makes a poor architect. The Tarantula's murderess does not know how to dig a cell for her larva; she does not know how to fill up the entrance by sweeping dust into it. The first hole encountered at the foot of a wall contents her, provided that it be roomy enough; a little heap of rubbish will do for a door. Nothing could be more expeditious.

I withdraw the game from the hole. The egg is stuck to the Spider, near the beginning of the belly. A clumsy movement on my part makes it fall off at the moment of extraction. It is all over; the thing will not hatch; I shall not be able to observe the development of the larva. The Tarantula lies motionless, flexible as in life, with not a trace of a wound. In short, we have here life without movement. From time to time the tips of the tarsi quiver a little; and that is all. Accustomed of old to these deceptive corpses, I can see in my mind's eye what has happened the Spider has been stung in the region of the thorax, no doubt once only, in view of the concentration of her nervous system. I place the victim in a box in which it retains all the pliancy and all the freshness of life, from the 2nd of August to the 20th of September, that is to say, for seven weeks.

The most important matter has escaped me. What I wanted, what I still want to see is the Pompilus engaged in mortal combat with the Tarantula. What a duel, in which the cunning of the one has to overcome the terrible weapons of the other! Does the Wasp enter the burrow to surprise the Tarantula at the bottom of her lair? Such temerity would be fatal to her. Where the big Bumble-bee dies an instant death, the audacious visitor would perish the moment she entered. Is not the other there, facing her, ready to snap at the back of her head, inflicting a wound which would result in sudden death? No, the Pompilus does not enter the Spider's parlour, that is obvious. Does she surprise the Spider outside her fortress? But the Tarantula is a stay-at-home animal: I do not see her straying abroad during the summer. Later, in the autumn, when the Pompili have disappeared, she wanders about; turning gipsy, she takes the open air with her numerous family, which she carries on her back. Apart from these maternal strolls, she does not appear to me to leave her castle; and the Pompilus, I should think, has no great chance of meeting her outside. The problem, we perceive, is becoming complicated: the huntress cannot make her way into the burrow, where she would risk sudden death; and the Spider's sedentary habits make an encounter outside the burrow improbable. Here is a riddle which it would be interesting to decipher. Let us endeavour to do so by observing other Spider-hunters; analogy will enable us to draw a conclusion.

I have often watched Pompili of every species on their hunting-expeditions, but I have never surprised them entering the Spider's lodging when the latter was at home. Whether this lodging be a funnel plunging its neck into a hole in some wall, an awning stretched amid the stubble, a tent modelled upon the Arab's, a sheath formed of a few leaves bound together, or a net with a guard-room attached, whenever the owner is indoors the suspicious Pompilus holds aloof. When the dwelling is vacant, it is another matter: the Wasp moves with arrogant ease over those webs and cables in which so many other insects would remain ensnared. The silken threads do not seem to have any hold upon her. What is she doing, exploring these empty webs? She is watching to see what is happening on the adjacent webs where the Spider is ambushed. The Pompilus, therefore, feels an insuperable reluctance to make straight for the Spider when the latter is at home in the midst of her snares. And she is right, a hundred times over. If the Tarantula understands the practice of the dagger-thrust in the neck, which is immediately fatal, the other cannot be unacquainted with it. Woe then to the imprudent Wasp who presents herself upon the threshold of a Spider of approximately equal strength!

Of the various instances which I have collected of this cautious reserve on the Spider-huntress' part I will confine myself to the following, which will be sufficient to prove my point. By joining, with silken strands, the three leaflets which form the leaf of Virgil's cytisus, a Spider has built herself a green arbour, a horizontal sheath, open at either end. A questing Pompilus comes upon the scene, finds the game to her liking and pops in her head at the entrance of the cell. The Spider immediately retreats to the other end. The huntress goes round the Spider's dwelling and reappears at the other door. Again the Spider retreats, returning to the first entrance. The Wasp also returns to it, but always by the outside. Scarcely has she done so, when the Spider rushes for the opposite opening; and so on for fully a quarter of an hour, both of them coming and going from one end of the cylinder to the other, the Spider inside and the Pompilus outside.

The quarry was a valuable one, it seems, since the Wasp persisted for a long time in her attempts, which were invariably defeated; the huntress had to abandon them, however, baffled by this perpetual running to and fro. The Pompilus made off; and the Spider, once more on the watch, patiently awaited the heedless Midges. What should the Wasp have done to capture this much-coveted game? She should have entered the verdant cylinder, the Spider's dwelling, and pursued the Spider direct, in her own house, instead of remaining outside, going from one door to the other. With such swiftness and dexterity as hers, it seemed to me impossible that the stroke should fail; the quarry moved clumsily, a little sideways, like a Crab. I judged it to be an easy matter; the Pompilus thought it highly dangerous. To-day I am of her opinion; if she had entered the leafy tube, the mistress of the house would have operated on her neck and the huntress would have become the quarry.

Years passed and the paralyser of the Spiders still refused to reveal her secret; I was badly served by circumstances, could find no leisure, was absorbed in unrelenting preoccupations. At length the light dawned upon me. My garden at Orange was enclosed by an old wall, blackened and ruined by time, where, in the chinks between the stones, lived a population of Spiders, represented more particularly by the common Cellar Spider, or Segestria.

She is deep black all over, excepting the mandibles, which are a splendid metallic green. Her two poisoned daggers look like a product of the metal-worker's art, like the finest bronze. In any mass of abandoned masonry there is not a quiet corner, not a hole the size of one's finger, in which the Segestria does not set up house. Her web is a widely flaring funnel, whose open end, at most a span across, lies spread upon the surface of the wall, where it is held in place by radiating threads. This conical surface is continued by a tube which runs into a hole in the wall. At the end is the dining-room to which the Spider retires to devour at her ease her captured prey.

With her two hind-legs stuck into the tube to obtain a purchase and the six others spread around the orifice, the better to perceive on every side the quiver which gives the signal of a capture, the Segestria waits motionless, at the entrance of her funnel, for an insect to become entangled in the snare. Large Flies, Drone-flies, dizzily grazing some thread of the snare with their wings, are her usual victims. At the first flutter of the netted Fly, the Spider runs or even leaps forward, but she is now secured by a cord which escapes from the spinnerets and which has its end fastened to the silken tube. This prevents her from falling as she darts along a vertical surface. Bitten at the back of the head, the Drone-fly is dead in a moment; and the Segestria carries him into her lair.

Thanks to this method and these hunting-appliances—an ambush at the bottom of a silken whirlpool, radiating snares, a life-line which holds her from behind and allows her to take a sudden rush without risking a fall—the Segestria is able to catch game less inoffensive than the Drone-fly. A Common Wasp, they tell me, does not daunt her. Though I have not tested this, I readily believe it, for I well know the Spider's boldness. This boldness is reinforced by the activity of the venom. Without being serious to man, the sting causes sharp pain and swelling. It must be a terrible thing for insects, whether because of the small size of the victim or because it acts with special efficacy upon an organisation which differs widely from our own. One Pompilus, though greatly inferior to the Segestria in size and strength, nevertheless makes war upon the Cellar Spider and succeeds in overpowering this formidable quarry. This is the Bee Pompilus, who is hardly larger than the Hive-bee and very much slenderer. She is of a uniform black; her wings are a cloudy brown, with transparent tips. Let us follow her in her expeditions to the old wall inhabited by the Segestria.

The Spider-huntress explores the wall minutely; she runs, leaps and flies; she comes and goes, flitting to and fro. The antennæ quiver; the wings, raised above the back, continually beat one against the other. Ah, here she is, close to a Segestria's funnel! The Spider, who has hitherto remained invisible, instantly appears at the entrance to the tube; she spreads her six forelegs outside, ready to receive the huntress. Far from fleeing before the terrible apparition, she watches the watcher, fully prepared to prey upon her enemy. Before this intrepid demeanour the Pompilus draws back. She examines the coveted game, walks round it for a moment, then goes away without attempting anything. When she has gone, the Segestria retires indoors, backwards. For the second time the Wasp passes near an inhabited funnel. The Spider on the look out at once shows herself on the threshold of her dwelling, half out of her tube, ready for defence and perhaps also for attack. The Pompilus moves away and the Segestria reenters her tube. A fresh alarm: the Pompilus returns; another threatening demonstration on the part of the Spider. Her neighbour, a little later, does better than this: while the huntress is prowling about in the neighbourhood of the funnel, she suddenly leaps out of the tube, with the life-line which will save her from falling, should she miss her footing, attached to her spinnerets; she rushes forward and hurls herself in front of the Pompilus, at a distance of some eight inches from her burrow. The Wasp, as though terrified, immediately decamps; and the Segestria no less suddenly retreats indoors.

Here, we must admit, is a strange quarry: it does not hide, but is eager to show itself; it does not run away, but flings itself in front of the hunter. If our observations were to cease here, could we say which of the two is the hunter and which the hunted? Should we not feel sorry for the imprudent Pompilus? Let a thread of the trap entangle her leg; and it is all up with her. The other will be there, stabbing her in the throat. What, then, is the method which she employs against the Segestria, always on the alert, ready for defence, audacious to the point of aggression? Shall I surprise the reader if I tell him that this problem filled me with the most eager interest, that it held me for weeks in contemplation before that cheerless wall? Nevertheless, my tale will be a short one.

On several occasions I see the Pompilus suddenly fling herself on one of the Spider's legs, seize it with her mandibles and endeavour to draw the animal from its tube. It is a sudden rush, a surprise attack, too quick to permit the Spider to parry it. Fortunately, the latter's two hind legs are firmly hooked to the dwelling; and the Segestria escapes with a jerk, for the other, having delivered her shock attack, hastens to release her hold; if she persisted, the affair might end badly for her. Having failed in this assault, the Wasp repeats the procedure at other funnels; she will even return to the first when the alarm is somewhat assuaged. Still hopping and fluttering, she prowls around the mouth, whence the Segestria watches her, with her legs outspread. She waits for the propitious moment; she leaps forward, seizes a leg, tugs at it and springs out of reach. More often than not, the Spider holds fast; sometimes she is dragged out of the tube, to a distance of a few inches, but immediately returns, no doubt with the aid of her unbroken life-line.

The Pompilus' intention is plain: she wants to eject the Spider from her fortress and fling her some distance away. So much perseverance leads to success. This time all goes well: with a vigorous and well-timed tug the Wasp has pulled the Segestria out and at once lets her drop to the ground. Bewildered by her fall and even more demoralized by being wrested from her ambush, the Spider is no longer the bold adversary that she was. She draws her legs together and cowers into a depression in the soil. The huntress is there on the instant to operate on the evicted animal. I have barely time to draw near to watch the tragedy when the victim is paralysed by a thrust of the sting in the thorax.

Here at last, in all its Machiavellian cunning, is the shrewd method of the Pompilus. She would be risking her life if she attacked the Segestria in her home: the Wasp is so convinced of it that she takes good care not to commit this imprudence; but she knows also that, once dislodged from her dwelling, the Spider is as timid, as cowardly as she was audacious at the centre of her funnel. The whole point of her tactics, therefore, lies in dislodging the creature. This done, the rest is nothing.

The Tarantula-huntress must behave in the same manner. Enlightened by her kinswoman, the Bee Pompilus, my mind pictures her wandering stealthily around the Spider's rampart. The Tarantula hurries up from the bottom of her burrow, believing that a victim is approaching; she ascends her vertical tube, spreading her forelegs outside, ready to leap. But it is the Ringed Pompilus who leaps, seizes a leg, tugs it and hurls the Spider outside her burrow. She is henceforth a craven victim, who will let herself be stabbed without dreaming of employing her venomous fangs.

Two contrasting points impress me in the facts which I have just set forth: the shrewdness of the Pompilus and the folly of the Spider. I will admit that the Wasp may gradually have acquired, as being highly beneficial to her posterity, the instinct by which she first of all so judiciously drags the victim from its refuge, in order there to paralyse it without incurring danger, provided that you will explain why the Segestria, possessing an intellect no less gifted than that of the Pompilus, does not yet know how to counteract the trick of which she has so long been the victim. What would the Cellar Spider need to do to escape her exterminator? Practically nothing: it would be enough for her to reenter her tube, instead of coming up to post herself at the entrance like a sentry, whenever the enemy is in the neighbourhood. It is very brave of her, I agree; but it is also very risky. The Pompilus will pounce upon one of the legs spread outside the burrow for defence and attack; and the besieged Spider will perish, betrayed by her own boldness. This posture is excellent when waiting for prey. But the Wasp is not a quarry: she is an enemy and one of the most dread of enemies. The Spider knows this. At the sight of the Wasp, instead of posting herself fearlessly but foolishly on her threshold, why does she not retreat into her fortress, where the other would not attack her? The accumulated experience of generations should have taught her this elementary tactical device, which is of the greatest value to the prosperity of her race. If the Pompilus has perfected her method of attack, why has not the Segestria perfected her method of defence? Is it possible that centuries upon centuries should have modified the one to its advantage without succeeding in modifying the other?

Let us return to the habits of the Bee Pompilus. Without expecting results of any particular interest, for in captivity the respective talents of the huntress and the quarry seem to slumber, I place together, in a wide jar, a Wasp and a Segestria. The Spider and her enemy mutually avoid each other, both ben equally timid. A judicious shake or two brings them into contact. The Segestria, from time to time, catches hold of the Pompilus, who gathers herself up as best she can, without attempting to use her sting; the Spider rolls the insect between her legs and even between her mandibles, but appears to dislike doing it. Once I see her lie on her back and hold the Pompilus above her, as far away as possible, while turning her over in her forelegs and munching at her with her mandibles. The Wasp, whether by her own adroitness or owing to the Spider's dread of her, promptly escapes from the terrible fangs, moves to a short distance and does not seem to trouble unduly about the buffeting which she has received. She quietly polishes her wings and curls her antennæ by pulling them while standing on them with her fore-tarsi. The attack of the

Segestria, stimulated by my shakes, is repeated ten times over; and the Pompilus always escapes from the venomous fangs unscathed, as though she were invulnerable.

Is she really invulnerable? By no means, as we shall soon have proved to us: if she retires safe and sound, it is because the Spider does not use her fangs. What we see is a sort of truce, a tacit convention forbidding deadly strokes, or rather the demoralization due to captivity; and the two adversaries are no longer in a sufficiently warlike mood to make play with their daggers. The tranquillity of the Pompilus, who keeps on jauntily curling her antennæ in face of the Segestria, reassures me as to my prisoner's fate; for greater security, however, I throw her a scrap of paper, in the folds of which she will find a refuge during the night. She installs herself there, out of the Spider's reach. Next morning I find her dead. During the night the Segestria, whose habits are nocturnal, has recovered her daring and stabbed her enemy. I had my suspicions that the parts played might be reversed! The butcher of yesterday is the victim of to-day.

I replace the Pompilus by a Hive-bee. The interview is not protracted. Two hours later, the Bee is dead, bitten by the Spider. A Drone-fly suffers the same fate. The Segestria, however, does not touch either of the two corpses, any more than she touched the corpse of the Pompilus. In these murders the captive seems to have no other object than to rid herself of a turbulent neighbour. When appetite awakes, perhaps the victims will be turned to account. They were not; and the fault was mine. I placed in the jar a Bumble-bee of average size. A day later the Spider was dead; the rude sharer of her captivity had done the deed.

Let us say no more of these unequal duels in the glass prison and complete the story of the Pompilus whom we left with the paralysed Segestria at the foot of the wall. She abandons her prey on the ground and returns to the wall. She visits the Spiders' funnels one by one, walking on them as freely as on the stones; she inspects the silken tubes, plunging her antennæ into them, sounding and exploring them; she enters without the least hesitation. Whence does she now derive the temerity thus to enter the Spiders' lairs? But a little while ago, she was displaying extreme caution; at this moment, she seems heedless of danger. The fact is that there is no danger really. The Wasp is inspecting uninhabited houses. When she dives down a silken tunnel, she very well knows that there is no one in, for, had the Segestria been there, she would by this time have appeared on the threshold. The fact that the householder does not show herself at the first vibration of the neighbouring threads is a certain proof that the tube is vacant; and the Pompilus enters in full security. I shall recommend future observers not to take the present investigations for hunting-tactics. I have already remarked and I repeat: the Pompilus never enters the silken ambush while the Spider is there.

Among the funnels inspected one appears to suit her better than the others; she returns to it frequently in the course of her investigations, which last for nearly an hour. From time to time she hastens back to the Spider lying on the ground; she examines her, tugs at her, drags her a little closer to the wall, then leaves her the better to reconnoitre the tunnel which is the object of her preference. Lastly she returns to the Segestria and takes her by the tip of the abdomen. The quarry is so heavy that she has great difficulty in moving it along the level ground. Two inches divide it from the wall. She gets to the wall, not without effort; nevertheless, once the wall is reached, the job is quickly done.

The Wasp hoists her prey backwards, her enormous prey, which dangles beneath her. She climbs now up a vertical plane, now up a slope, according to the uneven surface of the stones. She crosses gaps where she has to go belly uppermost, while the quarry swings to and fro in the air. Nothing stops her; she keeps on climbing, to a height of six feet or more, without selecting her path, without seeing her goal, since she goes backwards. Here is a ledge, no doubt reconnoitred beforehand and now reached, despite the difficulties of an ascent which did not allow her to see it. The Pompilus lays her prey on it. The silken tube which she inspected so lovingly is only some eight inches distant. She goes to it, examines it rapidly, and returns to the Spider, whom she at length lowers down the tube.

Shortly afterwards I see her come out again. She searches here and there on the wall for a few scraps of mortar, two or three fairly large pieces, which she carries to the tube, to close it up. The task is done. She flies away.

Next day I inspect this strange burrow. The Spider is at the bottom of the silken tube, isolated on every side, as though in a hammock. The Wasp's egg is glued not to the ventral surface of the victim but to the back, about the middle, near the beginning of the abdomen. It is white, cylindrical and about a twelfth of an inch long. The few scraps of mortar which I saw carried have but very roughly cut off the silken chamber at the end. Thus the Bee Pompilus lays her quarry and her eggs not in a burrow of her own making, but in the Spider's actual house. Perhaps the silken tube belongs to this very victim, which in that event provides both board and lodging. What a shelter for the larva of this Pompilus: the warm retreat and downy hammock of the Segestria!

Here then, already, we have two Spider-huntresses, the Ringed Pompilus and the Bee Pompilus, who, unversed in the miner's craft, establish their offspring inexpensively in accidental chinks in the walls, or even in the lair of the Spider on which the larva feeds. In these cells, acquired without exertion, they build only an attempt at a wall with a few fragments of mortar. But we must beware of generalizing about this expeditious method of establishment. Other Pompili are true diggers, who valiantly sink a burrow in the soil, to a depth of a couple of inches. These include the Eight-spotted Pompilus, with her black-and-yellow livery and her amber wings, a little darker at the tips. For her game she chooses the Garden Spiders, magnificently adorned, who lie in wait at the centre of their large, vertical webs. I am not sufficiently acquainted with her habits to describe them; above all, I know nothing of her hunting-tactics. But her dwelling is familiar to me: it is a burrow, which I have seen her begin, complete and close according to the customary method of the Digger-wasps.

# A WASTE-PAPER PHILOSOPHY
## (To My Son)


By T. P. Cameron Wilson[2]

WHEN a man begins to be certain he begins to be a fool. Nevertheless those moments in his life when he has seemed to catch a glimpse of truth may have had their value.

Here, my son, are some of the blurred things seen as I have jumped. In most of them the tangle of stalks and weeds was half between my eyes and the beauty of earth. I am a very little dog and I did not always jump. Also there were too many rabbits. And I am still in the corn.

I saw my Master once, standing by the gate, looking towards me. That was a long time ago...

And all this I thought and wrote in France, among the entanglements of war.


The most valuable thing in the world is a friend, and the next most valuable is another friend.

Make friendship as you would make a house, carefully and very surely. But do not acidly select your material, as a schoolmistress does. Be like Kim, "little friend of all the world." Only despise the man who loves people for their clothes, or money, or titles. The rest are your brothers. But many of them will despise you (unless you are successful, when they will hate you). And these you must pity, because they keep their windows shut.

A man must have something in his life more important than himself. Usually he has a wife. But that takes time and often money. Sometimes it is a book, or a motor bicycle, or a dog. But whatever it is a man is damned without it, because he lives then in the house of mirrors and will go mad (or blind) with the sheer horror of himself.

But above all is he happy if he thinks he knows something of God, and does not permit the evil of his own heart to scare away the thought of that great

---

[2] Killed in action, March 23, 1918.

Sympathy. For God must understand evil perfectly and know more evil things than you.

Now of God, argument is futile, though it may profit you to beat out a thought thereby, like a blade on an anvil.

If God exists, He is made of all beauty; and all beauty is but part of God. Colour and life and sun-washed air, wind, and the smell of wild mint on lonely hills, the love of women and small children, music and great tears, and the grace of healthy men, the lonely bravery of Christ and of all great men, friendship which cannot speak but in the grip of hands, the calling of birds...they are little threads in the stuff which is the mind of God.

And if God does not exist, or if He is to human thought utterly inconceivable, what have we lost by weaving all beauty into the idea of Someone who understands us? We have but given a sympathy and outside strength to the joy of living.

But what shall a man say of evil, of crime and filth and ugliness? Are we to believe that old legend of some huge Rebel against God? Are we to believe the more subtle dilution of ethics? Or is evil nothing at all, or at most a point of view?

Of my own experience I know that in the dim room of my mind—against all love of beauty, against all arranged plans and builded creeds, against love, and knowledge, and hope, and the full strength of my conscious will, something has risen and taken me by the throat and shaken the sense of God from me. I am willing to believe that this evil is conscious. And if evil does not, after all, exist, if it is some mysterious reflection or perversion of the nature of God, what have we lost by weaving all filth into the idea of someone who hates the beauty of living? What have we lost by writing down the failures, the sickening falls, the damned old weaknesses and shames, as due to a kind of huge and spiteful hatred?

We have but added a little to the very human joy of conquest.

And if suddenly you *know* that everything is utter vanity and that God is not, and that life is a blind alley, go quickly and get drunk, for then at least you will be human and little, and you may shake off from you the taint of those vasty cold hells which have no horizon, where nothing personal or thinking is except yourself, where life and death and love and hate are formless and imbecile, like one great Face, without eyes or nose or mouth, a thing to make you mad if you think of it long enough. Oh! get very drunk then, and near to the earth, for she is warm and fragrant. Lie sometimes on your back and stare at the stars, and when you are nearly mad with the horror of them, turn and tear apart the grass roots and bury your silly nose, like a dog, in the very stuff of earth. It is good physic and should heal you of that horror of immensity. For if God is very great He is also very little... And when you have done this go indoors and wash your nose and play a game of Bridge, lest you become a prig.

Pain is sometimes Heaven's kick at the hinder parts of man to wake up the fool. But sometimes it is a deep and awful mystery which little minds must leave alone, for pain is nearly always birth.

If ever you have to face death, to live for weeks expecting it hourly, you will be surprised how commonplace the prospect of it becomes. But if fear should come I counsel you to side-step from its bewildering blows. Do not try hastily to fix your mind on some ready-made philosophy or religion which shall stiffen you to meet your enemy, for fear has a way of scattering your marshalled thoughts and leaving you dry-mouthed and wet in the hand, with no defences. But concern yourself with something different from danger— either trivial or great. Lift a comrade or sharpen a pencil, and do it well and with all consciousness. It is for this that the aristocrats of the French Revolution made play before the guillotine with snuff boxes and canes. It is for this that the soldier lights his cigarette... And for your thoughts, think only of one thing steadfastly and let it be beautiful—a field, a woman, a wood at Springtime, a dog, rain over the hills, the smile of your friend, children, or little birds, or the mad sea, or silver drowned in a green, still water... Of your beastly past I pray you to forget it utterly, lest you make hastily a sort of repentant panic as a gloss for that which you know may not be forgiven by yourself and can only be pardoned by God, who is love. If you can think at all, hope. And so should death cut short your thinking—either you will sleep utterly or go forward, as a man should. For it is wise to think backward and forward, seeing life as a swift high-flying bird must see one field below. But if you have already—in more spacious hours—made for yourself a philosophy or religion which will withstand the shock of naked and bloody reality and not be shattered, then God has indeed been good to you, and you will die without greater difficulty than that offered by the body, which clings too naturally to continuity. God is never sudden. When the "Do this" or "Do that" of His destiny seems to you abrupt, remember that you have already done (or failed to do) what He requires, by the habit of your will. You have moved to an event. That is all. You have not been dropped into it from a celestial aeroplane. If you could look back you would see your path, and know that you chose it yourself.

God gives to each man, however beset he may be with the world, a few minutes at least daily, when he is utterly alone.

Always lead "a double life." Keep in your heart a secret room. In the midst of traffic, at tennis, in restaurants and offices, exult that there wait for you somewhere great ghosts of your own creation. And when you shut the door of your bedroom let them crowd round you—the splendid brothers of the mind. Then you will go out to the world again clothed head to foot in the armour of beauty that they have put on you in secret. And someone passing you in the street will catch benediction from you and go on his way not knowing why a glimpse at your eyes has made him almost merry in a world of little content. Moreover, when life slaps you in the face, you may remember your hid haven, and laugh at the rowdy world, and so go rejoicing, as a philosopher should, to the things that matter.

Let heaven sometimes sweat offence from you. If you feel grossness swell in you, let the sun burn it out and the rain wash you clean again.

When you go first into a room make it instantly a shrine, for if you live there it is well that you live with nothing ugly.

And thoughts clothe an empty room more certainly than wallpaper.

Do not fall too easily into the fallacy that a deed is somehow more final than a thought. It is neither more nor less than a step on a road, a link in a chain. To think that a line of thought is ended or broken by an act is as foolish as to suppose the chain of a necklace finished by the first bead it threads. There have been men who set themselves to build a wall of habit, let us say, in thinking, and who pushed an evil thought aside and went on with the building, but at an evil action threw down the trowel, gave themselves up as useless, and kicked their good work level with the mud again.

When you read, take the hammer of your brain and break apart all *clichés*. They are round-shot at the foot of thought, and lead you to suppose it dead. So you leave it to drown in seas of dreadful print, and Truth mourns another son.

When you pray I dare advise you break away from arranged titles, such as
the Church has hung round the neck of its God, though you may find some
of them more beautiful than any you can think yourself. But words such as
"Almighty" may drug the keenness of your senses when you try to touch God.
I have prayed to Him as the Great Calm Spirit, as Father, as King, as Friend,
and all the titles meant nothing, and fluttered like dead leaves on to the moving
stream of love...

Once, as I walked along a road I spoke to Him as the Splendid Friend, and
saw the huge sea, green and silent against the clouds, and near me the laughing
pines, and very far away a sail like a speck of foam, but which was a great ship,
full of men. And I knew I was a fool, and could not call Him anything, but
said, "Make me big, and less a fool"; and then I ran, and met my friends and
linked an arm through the warm arm of one and sang a silly song.

*(To be continued.)*

# "INCOMPLETE"

## By K. Balbernie

... "I, ALSO," said Gyas to his companion, on an autumn morning, when they walked in the country beyond Athens, "I also have been very near to loving a woman. Hence I do not speak entirely without knowledge. Moreover, when I say that the woman was the Athenian Cynthia, of whom report will have spoken even to you—"

"Ah, but to all Athens," returned Charicles, laughing; "truly, you philosophers have an original manner of loving!"

"I did not say I loved her," exclaimed his friend, with considerable heat. "You who are my fellow-student in the Academy should know it is not possible to love such a woman."

"Is she not beautiful, then, O Gyas? But it seems to me I have heard report speak otherwise."

"She is worse than beautiful, for she makes one curious, and sets a fever in the blood. I do not know even the exact colour and shape of her eyes, because of the eternally changing lights in them, which confuse my thought. And there is that about her lips, even mocking, and the fall of her garments, that drives one to carnal imagination."

"If only the memory of her so agitates you, my poor Gyas," said Charicles, gravely, "you did well for your mind's peace to flee from her in time."

"I am far from agitated, and would entreat you not to believe I fear her. Such an emotion, for so slight a thing, is beneath the dignity of a wise man."

"It must be a great comfort to know yourself so wise," said Charicles, with courtesy; "and that you are heated is doubtless due to the sun, which seems always untempered on these country highways, even softened by the breath of autumn."

"Yes, indeed," replied Gyas with alacrity; "and besides, I doubt if we showed wisdom in selecting a day of the Lesser Dionysia for our own diversion. Everywhere one fears to come upon the disturbing procession of the bacchanals—"

"I know, I know," agreed the other, sympathetically; "With the ivy-garlands, and wild music, and the symbols...

"It is all very well in Athens," said Gyas, "where one may remain a spectator. But in these primitive places... That last village we passed through?"

"Anaphlystus."

"It was terrible! Smelling all of dust and trampled grapes. And—hark!— the clamour of the 'Io! Io Bacche!' is ringing faintly in our ears yet!"

"You are right, Gyas; it is terrible. Let us turn aside by this path over the fields, and, sitting there in the austere shadow of yonder cypress, talk no more of music, and maddening beauty...and oh, no more of love!"

But Gyas, retiring to the tranquillity he liked so well, was complaisant.

"You must understand," he said, "I do not despise love. Indeed, in time I shall marry; as I consider it is every man's duty to give legitimate heirs to his state. But the maiden I choose for my wife will be virtuous, unsophisticated, and affectionate within the bounds of modesty. Thus love will naturally lose the undue prominence that poets and other ill-balanced persons assign to it, and make way for the other more important forces—"

"Which are...?"

"Ambition...the higher mathematics...sociology...statesmanship... Well, but, my good Charicles, can you not supply definitions for yourself? And do you not see how a true wife, such as I have described, would gladly admit her comparative insignificance beside all these great objects? Whereas, such a woman as... let us say, then, the Athenian Cynthia, would count an empire well lost for one night of the voluptuousness of which she knows all secrets!"

"You have never..." began the listener, tentatively.

"The gods forbid!" cried Gyas, growing pale. "But I have seen men whom she allured to their doom. Mighty men, O Charicles, some of them wise once as I am now. And some died; and all were as mad with the desire of her!"

"You will never be punished for a vicarious sin," said Charicles, but so softly that Gyas heard him not.

Instead, this latter pursued:

"Without her, they might have gone on in their clean and lofty manhood. But with all the wiles she knew; her mouth on their mouth, her body... Oh, Charicles, what pardon should there be for such a woman? What pity? She is but the instrument of passion, and when we consider this passion, how wanton and devastating a thing—"

But they had now come into the shadow of the ebon tree, and when his companion said, seriously, "Do you still wish to speak of Cynthia?" Gyas answered with dignity:

"I did not wish to speak of her at all, and will certainly not profane the repose of this place with the echo of her name."

"In that case," said Charicles, seating himself on the deep grass under the cypress, "let us discourse, like true men, on the higher mathematics."

Late that evening, in the warm and aromatic room where Cynthia held her lover on her breast in a mood of tenderness, she whispered in a smile, "And what else did the wise man tell you, my Charicles, in the pure air beyond Anaphlystus?"

"Kiss me," he pleaded, "and I will tell you."

"You shall kiss me," she said, "when you have told me!"

"My darling, I cannot tell you, for I did not listen!"

Cynthia laughed:

"But you know he was wise!"

He pressed his lips on hers.

# THE WAR-POETRY OF SOLDIER POETS

## By Vero W. Garratt

SOLDIER poets are the true historians of the war. Unlike the host of professional versifiers who sat up day and night on Parnassus, pouring out their patriotic zeal in allegorical rhymes of battles and batteries with more than Æsopian facility, the soldier poets have given to life and literature a genuine interpretation of warfare stripped bare of artificiality.

And here I would suggest at the outset that, apart from literary considerations, these poets have done an immense service to humanity in "breaking forth light and truth" on the mist of deceit and misrepresentation that was thrown up between the public's mind and the experience of men in the trenches. The pity is that the mist is so thick that it is almost impossible to penetrate it.

As the majority of people know little of warfare in its real sense, the poetry of soldier poets may be thought to lack the appeal, or, by its absolute downrightness, to be somewhat misunderstood.

But if it fulfils the function of poetry by presenting an aspect of life in accordance with metrical composition neither of those conditions should stand. If it does lack the appeal, it is more because of the truths it unfolds than of any inherent failure to instruct or give pleasure. If it is misunderstood, all that is signified is that the emotions and experience it portrays are too abnormal and severe for easy appreciation, and requires a "stepping out" of the ordinary current of life.

And in so far as this is true the poetry is not likely to live. Indeed it would be thwarting the intentions of Mars and his host to allow these bards to steal a little more fire from heaven, for the sake of the world's peace. They want another age of Kaspars to follow on the present, and therefore Peterkin must not be answered in terms of unofficial poetry.

And this gives the clue to the negative qualities of the work. It is poetry that is not ultra-patriotic. It is not saturated with red, white and blue, nor blatant with extravagant national pride.

Whitehall is never mentioned. The word "patriot" does not occur once in the whole anthology I have before me.[3] But this does not imply the absence of real intensive patriotism of the poets concerned. There are indeed many poems that reveal an exquisite tenderness for all national ties, but it is not the provocative patriotism let loose in the world like a wild beast that respects only its own craving. Rather is it the patriotism of one who loving all departs.

> A little sadly, strangely, fearfully,
> As one who goes to try a mystery;

or as Ivor Gurney thought of his beloved England,

> Now these are memories only, and your skies and rushy sky-pools,
> Fragile mirrors easily broken by moving airs;
> But deep in my heart for ever goes on your daily being
> And uses consecrate.

There is also an entire absence of hate. That the most malicious feelings should have been cultivated by the people least directly concerned with the enemy, sheds an instructive light on war-time psychology. If civilian poets could not write a Hymn of Hate, they were less inclined to write a Hymn of Love, and it is indeed refreshing to remember that at a time when the gospel of hate was being preached at its highest, Hamilton Sorley was addressing Germany as early as 1915 in the following strain:—

> You are blind like us. Your hurt no man designed,
> And no man claimed the conquest of your land.
> But, gropers both through fields of thought confined,
> We stumble and we do not understand.
> You only saw your future bigly planned,
> And we, the tapering paths of our own mind,
> And in each other's dearest ways we stand,
> And hiss and hate. And the blind fight the blind.
> When it is peace, then we may view again
> With new-won eyes each other's truer form,
> And wonder. Grown more loving-kind and warm,

---

[3] "The Muse in Arms." By E. B. Osborn. John Murray. *7s. 6d.* net.

> We'll grasp firm hands and laugh at the old pain,
> When it is peace. But, until peace, the storm,
> The darkness, and the thunder and the rain.

Truly a genuine reminder that the Peace Treaty did not come from the stuff of which poets are born.

The truth is that soldier poets were too intimate with the thoughts and feelings of fighting men to represent them as crimson-eyed and hectic, with the divine fury of a Fleet Street office.

Neither is this poetry aflame with the so-called glory of warfare. The sentiment that fixed an aureole around every young fellow's head so long as he had enough strength to pull a trigger or stab a body, gains little support from writers who knew the reality of having to do these things. The mantle of Sidney might be pleasant to wear in a comfortable plush armchair, but it lost much of its traditional romance in the trenches. To imagine, as so many people have done, that young men full of the joy and the glory of life plunged into the horrors of battle with the zest of one taking a rose-water bath, is to miss the almost pathetic note of a poem like "Love of Life," written by John Street before going into action:—

> Reach out thy hands, thy spirit's hands, to me
> And pluck the youth, the magic from my heart—
> Magic of dreams whose sensibility
> Is plumed like the light; visions that start
> Mad pressure in the blood: desire that thrills
> The soul with mad delight: to yearning wed
> All slothfulness of life; draw from its bed
> The soul of dawn across the twilight hills.
> Reach out thy hands, O spirit, till I feel
> That I am fully thine; for I shall live
> In the proud consciousness that thou dost give,
> And if thy twilight fingers round me steal
> And draw me unto death—thy votary
> Am I, O life; reach out thy hands to me.

The Raemaekers of poetic literature, Siegfried Sassoon, may be too realistic for many tastes, but nevertheless anyone who has had the

<blockquote>sweat of horror in his hair,</blockquote>

and

<blockquote>Climbed through darkness to the twilight air,<br>
Unloading hell behind him step by step,</blockquote>

will realise the force of his compositions in carrying out what Wordsworth might have done had he been in khaki m Flanders.

The marvel is that the Muse was able to keep its head erect amid the devastation and unholy contradictions of true poetic impulse. The trenches scarcely invited that "spontaneous overflow of powerful feelings" in the finest sense, but happily such poems as "The Rainbow," by Leslie Coulson, show how weak the circumstances could be to the spirit.

<blockquote>I watch the white dawn gleam,<br>
To the thunder of hidden guns.<br>
I hear the hot shells scream<br>
Through skies as sweet as a dream,<br>
Where the silver dawn-break runs.<br>
And stabbing of light<br>
Scorches the virginal white.<br>
But I feel in my being the old high sanctified thrill,<br>
And I thank the gods that the dawn is beautiful still.</blockquote>

But one could quote indefinitely. The "ghostly company" of brilliant young writers whose "silence is now a menace" in the fashioning of a better world, has passed on the soul of the trenches in all its nakedness. That this will be unrecognised by those who see a more desirable method of perpetuating the spirit of the war through the popularising of barren communiqués and "worked-up" documents is a sound reason why people should protect soldier war-poetry, and make it an influence in moulding the future. In it we have truth combined with beauty of expression; a dignified restraint; an heroic "standing by" the refinements of human nature, and a frank denial of all assumptions that represent war as anything less than a hideous, despoiling monster.

If we return will England be
Just England still to you and me?
The place where we must earn our bread?
We who have walked among the dead,
And watched the smile of Agony,
And seen the price of liberty
Which we have taken carelessly
From other hands. Nay, we shall dread,
        If we return,

Dread lest we hold blood-guiltily
The things that men have died to free.
Oh English fields will blossom red
For all the blood that has been shed
By men whose guardians are we,
        If we return.

# "SILLY-POINT"

## By S. O.

IF "nothing succeeds like excess," then success is secondary—which would seem to be the right way of looking at the present orgy of games, in truth the full business of the community. Like Kipling's "Boots, boots, boots," games are the refrain, games everywhere, games all the time, and seemingly nothing else matters from coal to the Coalition. The fair is furious and the fun is grim earnest. This summer the country is clearly of no mind but for ball hunting in one form or another, and Europe can go to perdition so long as we don't lose all the "tests" and the Americans don't win the rubbers at polo, tennis, golf, and next month there is the Carpentier-Dempsey fight. August is holidays. September, O, the shooting begins!

It is, of course, the reaction—the release, and it may be the highest philosophy, for nothing absolutely matters, and perhaps the cheapest way out of the horrors confronting us is to pretend that they don't exist and to go on playing, even if incidentally this happened to be Nero's method. In part it is politics feverishly encouraged by the Press—to take people's minds off the depreciating investments, dividends, war policies, etc., and prepare them for the autumn "slam." It may be entirely wholesome. As an expression it is sanity. We play while Europe screams. Thus we escape.

This is where psycho-analysis comes in. Take Lord's. In 1914 Lord's was "off." You strolled in, you sauntered out. Cricket was controversial. "Wanted livening up" kind of thing, and women were shamelessly and wholeheartedly bored. Now picture that awful Saturday, June 11. A mob. The West and the East ends. Women by the thousands. Frantic flappers. A wild scrimmage. Accommodation absurdly inadequate. No drinks. No stewards. Lord's looking like the scene at the Cup tie, and all London hanging on the result.

What has happened? Has London suddenly become cricket-mad? Was this mob composed of cricketers? Of course not. The explanation is the "stunt." These were sightseers, not cricketers. It is the under-stratum moving up, for the war has been a great leveller, and the thing now is the holiday, the sensation, the spectacle. Same as Mary Pickford, or Charlie. It is democracy thrusting through, and, don't forget, the winner of the golf amateur championship is an artisan.

I think that's it, that plus war and the cerebration left by war. No longer is Lord's a fashionable tea-ground. No more are the M.C.C. the complete jury. The tests are ours nationally. The Press are "all out" with the tide. It is almost dangerous to discuss the true side in a railway carriage. As a chap said to me when I suggested the propriety of allowing the Australians a day's rest before a "test," "it's lucky you're not in Yorkshire."

And as Lord's was nerves, so was our cricket. Yes, siree! Too much correct style. What at school we called "poking." To see the Australians playing a "silly-point" in a test on a plumb wicket is disquieting. Jolly odd! Mr. Gregory is no Spofforth. "Archie" Maclaren would not have played Armstrong as if he were obsessed. The eleven of forty-five millions ought to beat that of four millions any day, and the war applied to both. So minded, putting Nottingham down to our traditional "bad" start, the new crowd which thronged Lord's to enjoy itself got quite "hipped" at the tameness of the sight, for at the "Electric" the hero never fails and the new crowd hails from the films.

Probably, Wimbledon too will be besieged, and the "test" polo matches. What are we going to do about it?

One new element is woman. Girls to-day are brought up in their schools like boys. They play their games. They know all about cricket. They simply adored Woolley. Mr. Punch's jokes about "mamma" at Lord's are indecently out-of-date. The tens of thousands of women who have made shells and bombs have the taste now of "sports." Enthusiasm is high. The maiden over is not popular.

The wars in Europe, the economic prospects, the declining purchasing-power, who cares? Games are "stunts," and the stunt is the thing, the big gate, the speculation on the result, the morbid craze for forgetfulness of the realities of life as it is and will be. And so the very thing we decided should not be again—inefficiency, amateurishness, mental aphasia—this has come back with a frenzy, and we are the playground of the Western world.

Are we to be its playboy—and emigrate? Or, is this the true philosophy? I cannot answer. In one sense certainly it denotes evasion, indifference, even unintelligence. Nor are these mob revivalisms likely to prove lasting as we grow poorer and man finds that he has to work harder. But this is economics, the new blasphemy.

I state the phenomenon. The war has taught men to move about. Restrictions have broken down. Restlessness is chronic. Demos is "all over the ground" and it means to see all the sights that are and—criticise. Perhaps the simple explanation is relativity. This is how we deflate. It is our process of settling down. Don't think, play, win or lose. True, it does seem a pity that we cannot find a great bowler, if cricket is to be the supreme occupation. To find a Lohmann! We must have this potential somewhere. That is what we want, he and a champion heavy-weight.

Anyhow we ought not to complain. Youth is trumps, and we really are having a seasonable time. Not idle enough to read. Games all the way. No rain so far, and never mind the potatoes. England is throwing off the habit of war. We are returning to the plough. If the Poles or the Greeks disturb our search for a bowler, let them beware of "Lord's" in its ex-khaki asseveration.

# IRELAND BEFORE THE IMPERIAL COUNCIL

By Austin Harrison

NOW that the Colonial Premiers are assembled on these shores, and from behind the veil of secrecy with which State affairs are more and more shrouded we gather that the main problem is interdependence, it would seem fitting enough to make some use of this machinery to rid ourselves of the blood feud of Ireland, seeing that the policy of an eye for an eye, for all that it is in the Bible, holds out small prospect of success either for us or the Irish. For here we are up against a cultural problem of peculiar concern to our civilisation. To the average Englishman, Ireland represents a recurrent nightmare. He is not interested. He sees in this age-long periodic rebellion a challenge which, because it is not based upon hardship of governance other than that provoked by sentimental idealism, he regards as insolent, as something hardly to be mentioned in decent society. Characteristically, the subject, being unpleasant, annoys him. He ascribes it to the wayward Irish temperament, to bigotry, to insubordination. And this is the abominable difficulty. The Irish are idealists, we are practical politicians. We resent the poet republican. Ireland is prosperous enough, what more can Ireland want? The Irish therefore are "idiots." If idiots take to assassination, counter-assassination is the constable's reply. Seen thus, Ireland becomes a boil, an absurdity. It is this hopelessness of attitude, which is really unimaginativeness, that governs the despair of men so intellectually apart as A. E. in Ireland, and Sir Hamar Greenwood directing military operations in the cause of Ulster.

Were Ireland a simple national question, were the issue solely one of self-government or union, no doubt Carson and Valera, or Greenwood and Devlin, could find a working formula, for militarily Ireland can no longer be a danger to this country, and it is discreditable to intelligent soldiers, notably Ulstermen, that this "bogey" should still be dangled before the eyes of the British public bored stiff with the whole business. But this is only half the issue. The inside problem is not insular, it is secular, and it is now politically hopelessly complicated by the difference of opinion within the Church, virtually split on a basic point of spiritual strategy. This is what Irishmen mean when they bafflingly speak about Ireland as the "Faith" when they hasten to assure us that Ireland "never can be settled," as St. Patrick is reputed to have ordained. Even a man so wise and temperate as A. E. in his recent essay apparently shares this view, which is perilously akin to fatalism; yet if so, then fatalism is England's opportunity. For to assume impossibility is to abdicate, is to deny, reason; if so, then the Irish war is normal and reasonable, and for the Irish to complain is illogical. This we cannot accept. On the contrary, we have advanced. The Partition idea is recognised to be no solution, which means that the Irish problem must be viewed as a whole, as integrally an Irish insulation. This is progress. Partition implies the continuance and accentuation of Border politics, of Border economics, or Border Church rivalries, and on those lines peace is not obtainable. Far better a new plantation or Catholic expulsion policy, both of which however would serve but to make the Irish question more international in scope and more culturally degrading; both therefore can be ruled out. There is another way; to look upon Ireland imperially—that is, to treat the disease as a common responsibility, as an issue of that interdependence which will constitute the basis of our future imperial consanguinity.

The significance to us of Ireland is moral, and clearly if we cannot solve this problem of self-government there must be a strange weakness in our civilisation. On our side the trouble is far more resentment at the notion of yielding independence than the fact itself, which we granted with signal success to the Boers and indeed recognise to-day, as the result and price of the Great War, must henceforth govern the imperial idea as the sweet reasonableness of its continuity. Interdependence is the new constructive nexus, as we can see in the cases of Canada and Australia. The Tetrarch of Downing Street is no more, and even in India and Egypt success will ultimately depend upon the recognition of this principle and its application, and we shall ignore this sign at our peril. Here Ireland integrates. Domestically, we have failed, but we have not yet tried imperially. It is well worth our consideration. Ireland has come to be an English-speaking sore, a thing we avoid discussing, yet a cry we cannot smother. It blunts our world policy, sours our association with America. It offends our truest friends. Our progress is crossed, our proud name is besmirched; we can in no wise direct a League of

Peoples while manifesting our incompetence to settle our own affairs intelligently. And this indifference harms us throughout the world. We are not making good. In refusing to see in Ireland any issue but force, we are disintegrating.

It would be self-deception for us to imagine that Admiral Sims voiced a new American feeling in the bluff words which provoked his recall—these things are politics. Ireland is more than politics, it is a test of civilisation. To remove this canker, greatness is necessary, above all, trust, and it is because neither side trusts the other that the deadlock is so complete. True, we cannot yield to murder. Loathsome as is the Irish murder campaign, that is not the real difficulty, for all force is but a means, and in time that too will stop. What then? Shall we be any nearer to a solution? Nor is it truly the Republican idea at which we boggle—we never gave the Irish even the promised rose-water Home Rule. The root problem is the Church and the dissensions within a Church which fears Irish freedom from ecclesiastical authority, and it is here that England can boldly step in—with right and for the right. The Republican idea is mainly a flag. Ireland without England would economically perish. Ireland is one of our greatest buyers and lives by selling to us. Economically, the ties are mutual and assured. The idea of freedom is insular and derives from the sea, but to us its acceptance lies culturally in association. What does it matter to us if Ireland levies and collects her own taxes and governs herself? We do not impound half the taxation revenue of Australia, of South Africa. Why should we treat Ireland so churlishly? This is nationally the issue. A free Ireland need not imply a hostile Ireland. On the contrary, freedom would disarm her hostility; if only because she would have no wrong to nurse, her abstract grievance would dissolve; in the positive results of responsibility Sinn Fein would quickly socialise into a harmony founded on sound economic relationship. It is the fatalism which identifies Faith as the white star of fighting Ireland which presents the inner complex of peace, and this, if there is faith in us, we can surely face imperially, as the index of our justification. Reprisals will not help us. To the Arabs we send Lawrence, a statesman; to Ireland we send Black and Tans. Are the Irish not worth the new Jerusalem? Are the Egyptians to have a Home Rule denied to the Irish? Is India to be graduated into self-government yet not Ireland? We are not confronted with the problem of Henry IV of France, the peace of Ireland does not depend upon our reconversion. Precisely the contrary. Free Ireland, and Ireland will free herself. Trust Ireland, and Ireland will trust us. Give the Irish self-government, and they will emancipate themselves, and it may well be laïcise their politics—which is, of course, the reason of Rome's opposition to a free democratic Ireland. If we only realised the sanctuary offered through political freedom, we would grant the Irish all that they want forthwith; we would help them to democratise education, to become a responsible nation, to free themselves of their "devils and bedevilments," to align themselves with the imperial spirit. But this we shall not accomplish through force, for greater than force is their Faith, in which cause death is heralded as salvation.

To meet their Faith we must give them our Faith, if of a different blend. Yet that is the essential. The Irish are not unreasonable, they are logical, like the French, and this native simplicity is their strength. "To die for Ireland"— what does it mean? Yet it is the Irishman's constant prayer. It is a superstition, a legacy, a sacrament. Were we all Catholics, this fervour would collapse, but we can be Catholic in our treatment, even as Mahomet went to the mountain. Irish gunmen would speedily throw down their arms, were we to show a larger Faith, the faith of one democracy in another. The communion of brotherhood is a greater thing than a community of saints—with an historical grievance. What we have to purge out of Ireland is the snake in the grass, and blow in the oxygen of responsibility. If that method provoked dissension, then the Irish must fight it out among themselves, as probably they would. Well, the world would judge. We should have done our part. It is because we are not doing our part that the world not unnaturally judges us. On the lines of Ulster *versus* the rest, the plantation *versus* the rebels, or Catholic *versus* Protestant, Ireland will remain the absurd plague-spot in our midst and the breeding-ground of imperial dissociation. Not because of the national idea which is a human right, and so susceptible of adjustment, but because of the impersonal idealism which is the Irish genius and religion. A people of logical poets, as the Irish are, bounded by the seas, nursing the wrongs of centuries, cultivating a hate, a history, an insularity and a rosary, defy the blandishments of mere politics or all reason save that of the heart, which reason often does not know. Their landmarks are the "martyrs." To go on fabricating martyrs, thus increasing the "saintliness" of old Ireland, whether they be common assassins or not, is only to increase the sale of martyr post cards, to add to the snakes and dissensions, to solidify the unreason of our predicament which lies chiefly in our refusal to understand it. Yet a very slight comprehension of the purgatorial idea would convince even the sceptical among us of the futility of Tanks when Faith is the argument, where not Englishmen as Englishmen but the authority of Englishmen is the fighting and spiritual patriotism. If the patriotism denoted hostility between England and Ireland and implied implacable hostility in the event of our loosening our hold over the island, we might accept war as inevitable; but this is not so, as any man can satisfy himself who goes to Ireland even to-day on a holiday. What we are fighting for is Ulster ensconced in English Toryism; Ulster's claim, through England, to hold down Catholic Ireland, and were we Germans or Frenchmen the problem would be identical. When the Ulster leader recently saw Valera, this aspect must have been comically uppermost in their respective minds: it is a great pity that some Englishman was not present. Our question now is to decide whether we are willing to incur the world's opprobrium for this Border feud, or whether, in the interests of our civilisation, we intend to move forward to a fuller meaning of our imperialism implied surely in inner harmony and a truer co-operative dismembership. History is a better guide than provincialism, which latter is the crux of the problem. Were Ireland 500 miles away she would have been freed a century ago: it is really because of her propinquity that we refuse her claim, because so near Ireland seems part, so to speak, of the Metropolitan Board of Works, as we look out upon our world-wide dimensions.

All the same she is a fourth dimension—she is the space in our union, in our allegiance, in our humanity, and to continue hammering at this empty citadel is no longer intelligent. The policeman governor will never placate idealist and effeminate Ireland, and even if we "clear up" the island she will break out afresh—in the New World, in our world across the seas, shaking our far-flung Republics. Let us remember who destroyed Parnell—it was the Irish. That is the clue to the "mystery." It was the "you will never settle Ireland" idea which killed Parnell, as it would kill Sinn Fein, which is a genuine national or democratic movement, and the mistake we are making is to play into the hands of the forces who would disrupt it for St. Patrick's curse—not for peace in this life, but for the indefinite abstract motive of strife for the next one. Understand that, and we are at grips with the real problem, which to-day is not so much Ulster as the Church political; is not Partition but democratisation; is not England *versus* Ireland, but Ireland within and without her own Church. The need to-day is of an Act of Grace. When, as they do, the Irish condemn us and at the same time insist that Ireland will "never be settled because of St. Patrick," we have there the philosophy of the Irish cause and of its solution. The remedy for the abstract fatalism of violence is not more violence, it is to place Ireland on the table at the Imperial Conference. Let the Irish problem be syndicated, as it were, removed from Metropolitan departmentalism. Let us say to the Premiers of the Colonies "This is an imperial problem, be it solved imperially," and at once the onus of our charge is removed. If the Empire cannot settle it, we shall never be able to; but the Empire can settle it. Its findings would be accepted at any rate by the world, and if the Irish refused such adjudication they would sign away their own case historically. Ireland would be *chose jugée*. We in turn should be shriven.

The mere fact of our willingness to abide by an imperial ruling would constitute a world act of immense importance and automatically the needed equation between Britain and America would be found. It would be the first testimony to the League of Nations idea, infinitely more crisp and inspiring than any contrivance of a covenant founded on the interests of possession, which crumbles at the first test. Nothing would be simpler than to put this machinery of arbitration into force. The Premiers are here, and their chief quest is interdependence. Each of them knows the Irish problem from "on the spot." To the entire Anglo-Saxon world, Ireland is the bugbear of policy growing in intensity with its velocity here, now degenerated into a shooting match which no statesmanship can justify. If this is all we can do after our vociferous proclamations about "justice," democracy, and what not, the "far-flung" dependencies could at least do no worse; at any rate they would try to do something, whereas we are not seriously trying, we are still envisaging Ireland as a conquest legacy, as a domestic difficulty coming under Scotland Yard jurisdiction, when in fact it is our specific racial stigma. The Premiers should be given full powers to summon Valera and his confederates before the bar, to hear them and to confront them with the other side, and to cross-examine the respective Churches. And the proceedings should be public. Let them hear what the Hierarchy have to say about Sinn Fein and Sinn Fein about the Hierarchy, and what Ulster has to say about both, and as preliminary evidence of good faith let the Black and Tans be recalled and their places taken by the Regular Army. It would prove an astonishing inquisition and a revelation to most Englishmen who sincerely believe that the Irish want to be ruled over by the German Emperor. We might find great Irish opposition, reluctance to "face the music," but that would weigh in our balance as sincere arbiters; we might possibly find the Colonial Premiers more inclined to harsh methods than we are, yet that is not likely, The point about such a tribunal would be its common-sense, which the world would not fail to appreciate. Afterwards, we could go our way in peace again, conscious that we had done the right thing. Even if it led nowhere we should be absolved. In America, Ireland would cease from troubling, for if the problem turned out to be purely "spiritual," specifically the torture of creed, the bone of contention would no longer be England, it would be relegated to the "merry-thought" of Ireland and to the limbo of casuistry. Can we not rouse ourselves to seek so practical a way out? Or are we destined to "reconquer" Ireland while here the English Orthodox Church "goes over" to Rome?

A. E.'s despairing pamphlet is not convincing; what is convincing is the silence of Cardinal Mannix, who came hither to carry the "flaming sword." His silence is the highest eloquence. It means that above Faith there stands policy, and such is the eternal paradox of the "other" island. English Catholicism is notably hostile to a free Ireland, as hostile as Carson himself, yet hardly for the same reasons. For exactly contrary reasons, Ulster is hostile to the Catholic Church, English Catholics are hostile to Irish nationalism. There is a difference, a marked difference. And so in Ireland we find the young priests nakedly Sinn Fein, the Hierarchy sternly reproving, and again the enquirer is nonplussed. What does this mean? It means that age takes longer views than youth, that enthusiasm for Ireland captivates and carries away the young priesthood but does not blind age to the "dangers" of an Ireland working out her own destiny on free progressive lines. These "dangers" are or should be England's gifts to Ireland. Quite distinct from the Nationalist idea, which the Hierarchy mildly tolerates within limits, the idea of a laïcised Irish democracy strikes at the foundation of the control symbolised in what the Irish term the "Faith," and so we find the higher powers in Ireland fiercely denunciatory of Valera, who has even demanded the right of political freedom from Church control. These are the things the Colonial Premiers would have to decide upon, for to rig up an autonomous *régime* in Ireland would be the work of any constitutional lawyer. No doubt to utter these things is what the Press would call controversial, but they are root, and we shall not progress in Ireland until we tackle them in the full light of publicity. For the whole atmosphere of Ireland is surcharged with mystery, secrecy, masonry, espionage, and—treachery. We are in the realm of stiletto politics. A man can go through Ireland yet see and hear nothing. Search, and in a day you can plumb the depths of subterranean intrigue more contradictory and unfathomable than the mysteries of ex-Tsarist Russia. The ingredients are the same. Secret societies, caves and partnerships are everywhere. The Sinn Fein Army is a phantom force. The women are fierce participants. Ardent Sinn Feiners will assure you that Valera is a "spy." Everyone becomes a spy. And yet there is a strange and splendid sincerity, a wonderful organisation, a fearless enthusiasm. This wretched tangle has grown up; like weeds in a garden, the roots are deep. Hoe, and you find still deeper roots; the effects are a cumulative process of suspicion, intrigue, plot and counterplot which leave the enquirer bewildered. Speak to a Black and Tan, and he tells his pathetic tale. "Whatever we do is wrong. Even when we are murdered we are in the wrong."

Is this quite fair upon our manhood? Have we here no higher responsibility towards these men who fought in the war than to send them out to carry out reprisals? Is this really all that a British Government, literally arbiter of the world, can aspire to? It is hard to credit such abnegation of statesmanship. When Sir Hamar announces that he is tranquillising Ireland, has he ever considered that bigotry thrives on persecution, and that rightly or wrongly the Irish see in Castle government an unjustifiable intrusion and humiliation? This is our responsibility. It is ridiculous to pretend that Ireland, who largely governs America, cannot govern herself, or that we should be a penny the worse if she did. True, submission is difficult, but we can afford the gesture unless Ireland is to be merely another dog-fight. The Irish may be wilful, preposterous, fanatical, impossible, and no policeman likes to admit to failure—all that may be granted. There still remains the wisdom, the expediency, the decency even of holding down a people, treating them like an alien race, and regarding them now as a joke, now as the historical whipping-boy for official Cromwellianism. We shall not shame them into righteousness by shaming ourselves. That is certain. But we can save them from themselves. We can vindicate our own sincerity. We can by the merest correction of attitude restrain and reform their attitude, not with soldiers but through responsibility, by referring the entire murder and political problem to the sagacity of an Imperial Court.

In a day we can remove the cause, which is our presence in Ireland as conquerors. As friends we should be welcome enough. Conquerors of what? Of Cork? Of poor old St. Patrick? Of this little island of old people and legendary fighting cats? There is nothing to conquer—we can only devastate and complete the ruin, which would be less than idiotic. Demolishing bricks and mortar is hardly constructive, nor is a war on milk and butter conducive to pacification. But when a typical Irish girl, with laughter shining out of her violet eyes, insists that "you never can settle Ireland," then the plain, blunt man, as we fondly image ourselves, should take her at her word and pass that privilege on to the Empire which has a definite interest in the attempt. Two excellent results would accrue. One is that if Ireland declines to belong to England, we should discover whether she would acknowledge the Empire—and she would—in which case the arbitrament would be Imperial and the problem, so far as we are concerned, would be solved. The other is the grace that would come to us in the eyes of God and man from so magnanimous a confidence. To let the opportunity go by would be calamitous. It is not the mentality of Ireland unbound that we need fear to-day, but rather the mentality of a world aghast at our unimaginativeness. Ireland is not a problem of force, it is a problem of culture, and if we fail to find a solution we shall proclaim our incapacity to move with the times; we shall have lost that priceless jewel, our own Faith, without which imperially there can be no health in us.

# STRAVINSKY AND THE PRAGMATIC CRITERION IN CONTEMPORARY MUSIC

By Leigh Henry

## MUSIC AND THE EMPIRIC NECESSITIES OF TO-DAY.

NO period since the Renaissance has been marked by such acceleration of thought and effort, impulse and action, as is manifest to-day. Nor is the comparison confined to correspondences purely spiritual. As the Revival of Learning brought the consciousness of mediæval Europe into touch with unsuspected facts, and as astronomy and exploration modified its conception of the material universe, and replaced with saner reasoning the long-dominant credulity, so the scientific researches and inventions of the last century have made us aware of hitherto unknown forces, while the political, economic, and ethical exigencies of the late war have brought into being new conceptions of civilisation. On all sides, and in every department of contemporary life, there is a growing realisation of the universal need of new scales of values, new standards, and of new objectives and the practical methods by which to attain them. Everywhere there is a swelling, reiterated outcry, demanding reconstruction. Those responsible for the perpetuation of the old order of things, and those dependent upon its maintenance for their sanctions and privileges, endeavour to interpret this demand as an expression of the necessity for restoration; but, by slow, painful degrees, the significance of the experience undergone in the ghastly holocaust, and in its less dramatic but equally grim resultant tragedies, has filtered through the sediment of physical agony and spiritual weariness, and is infusing the consciousness of humanity with a realisation of the fundamental discrepancy which existed between the old theoretical standards and concepts, and the spiritual and material actualities of life. It is gradually becoming recognised that the foundations of what we have accepted as civilisation were too unsound to bear even the artificial and superficial structure of conventional existence which it was attempted to create upon them—too unsubstantial to undergo intact the physio-psychological processes of material and spiritual evolution. Everywhere scepticism is rife, extending to the established institutions, the conceptions upon which they are based, and the ideals for which they stand. The Revival of Learning clove asunder the shackles of religious superstition which bound the mentality of the Middle Ages, and opened up the way to rationalism. The modern developments of science, and the unprecedented exigencies of the war, and post-war, periods, have germinated a positive and practical type of thought which, in its turn, is destroying the obsessed reverence for pedagogy, pedantry, and abstract theory which, perverting the true vital nature of the Renaissance, persisted to a heavy culmination in the last century. It has become manifest that the theories and concepts upon which were based the values and conventions postulated by the old European standards of civilisation do not agree with the facts ascertained by experience, or the results produced by the changes resultant upon the action of physical phenomena and the evolution of the human sensibility and mind.

With such realisation the value of the old precedents ceases to exist. It becomes necessary to re-examine and analyse all the accepted values anew, in order to establish a working criterion for the reconstruction of our conceptions of life, and our means for encountering and coordinating its forces. To the attainment of this, abstract theory and philosophic speculation render little assistance. The emergencies of to-day are dominated by necessities not philosophic, but empiric. Habit, prejudice, and sentimental bias and association alike must be put aside: the phenomena of the present demand objective scrutiny, experiment, and investigation without premise,—in short, a pragmatic attitude of mind which will enable us to apprehend the facts of existence, their nature and relativity clearly and rationally, and render possible our formulation, organisation, and application of empirically justified methods with which to deal effectively, utilise, and develop their potentialities.

Music, as every other art, is a spiritual record of the vicissitudes of which political and economic history present the material aspects. Hence the present trend of consciousness is modifying its character to a markedly discernible degree. And in no other art has a rational and drastic revision of the governing standards and conventions been more imperatively required. The principles of form and construction upon which the conventional dogmas and practices of music have been based have been conceived, for the major part, in the most arbitrarily theoretical and abstract manner, quite apart from objective consideration of the essential nature and capacities of sound. Even the deductions made from the practices of the great musicians of the past have been halted by academic authority at a fixed point—the culmination of what is popularly designated "the classical period," and their contributions to the practical treatment of sound have been systematised into a collection of inhibitive formulæ. In all departments of musical construction extra-musical considerations have obscured the true nature of sound as a sensatory factor in human experience, extra-musical purposes have diverted it from its true functioning, that of stimulating and exercising the sensibility of humanity through aural channels. Theories, arbitrarily, or by loose analogy, derived from entirely extraneous spheres, such as those of architecture and mathematics, have superimposed stereotyped formulæ of craft—form, constructional detail, and design-balance or pattern—on the free treatment of the substance of sound, obscuring its natural qualities, and coercing them into channels too narrow for the spontaneous flow of its inherent expressive qualities. Added to this theoretical tyranny, music has been subordinated to purposes foreign to the nature of its own æsthetic qualities. Ethics, philosophy, literature, and graphic influences have successively imposed extraneous ideas, submerging its primary *raison d'être,* that of aural stimulation of a purely æsthetic state, beneath a mass of sentiments, associations, and emotional implications not intrinsic to its own identity as an art-medium. Thus it comes about that, while the substance of music has continued to develop, and to attain new capacities and potentialities of the aural sensation, the standards by which its constructive craftsmanship have been governed have remained within artificially restricted and stereotyped boundaries, and have thus eventually become obsolete in so far as their practical application to the necessities of sound creation are concerned.

The realisation of this underlies the new movement towards more positive methods apparent in varying degrees in all phases of contemporary musical activity—the movement tentatively essayed in the individualistic preoccupations of Impressionism, but there rendered abortive owing to the Impressionists' assumption of illustrative and sentimental implications, by being directed towards the secondary objective of suggestion instead of expression, and by the formulation of a tonal *cliché* of technical devices—

which finds its consummation in the new objective empiricism of Igor Stravinsky to-day.

## The Objective Æsthetic of Stravinsky.

Stravinsky is the first great musician to recognise, adopt, develop, and consistently postulate a direct objective treatment of the aural nature of sound in musical composition, apart from all intellectual premise or abstract theory. He has no musical dogma, but utilises his acute mentality to investigate, ascertain and co-ordinate the musical facts discerned by his extreme sensibility, or made apparent by his direct experiments with the aural nature of musical media. As a natural result of this objective concentration, it follows that he has no artificial technical limitations or conventions. The restrictions of modal melody and harmony, the diatonic, or tonic-central chromaticism, or the mathematically constructed scales and chord-systems which govern the works of the classic, the Romantics, and the Impressionists respectively, are never permitted to dominate in his work. For him music is not a question of tonalities and tonally-related harmonic progressions; it is a question of sonorous substance, of the musical *mot juste*, as implicit in the precise qualities of the note and of instrumental *timbre*. Stravinsky is practical, not theoretical; he has methods, but no hard-and-fast system. All the musical values of his work are derived from the intrinsic aural nature of sound-substance and sound-sensation treated as "things-in-themselves." By his methods he seeks to convey, not literary, graphic, or philosophic significances, or emotional implications suggested by means of mental association, but to present sensation in pure terms of sound-matter, to evoke what Jacques Copeau, of the Théâtre Vieux Colombier, terms *"un état de sensibilité."* As he himself has said:

"I want neither to suggest situations or emotions, but simply to manifest, to express them. I think there is in what are called 'Impressionist' methods a certain amount of hypocrisy, or at least a tendency towards vagueness or ambiguity. That I shun, above all things, and that perhaps is the reason why my methods differ as much from those of the Impressionists as they differ from academic conventional methods. Though I find it extremely hard to do so, I always aim at straightforward expression in its simplest form. I have no use for working-out in dramatic or lyric music. The one essential is to feel, and to convey one's feelings."

This clarity and eliminative trend follow naturally on Stravinsky's pragmatic criterion, derived from objective research into, and experiment with, the pure elements of musical fact, as ascertained sensatorily. The ethical, emotional, and poetic preoccupations of Romanticism, the subjective and suggestive implications of Impressionism, with their further superstrata of reflective thought, tended to obscure the essential nature of music, and obstruct the realisation of the intrinsic qualities of its aural substance. The music of Stravinsky, in impulse and content, as in technique, pertains to the domain of the actual, rather than to that of ideas. His works are the antithesis of metaphysical in every respect.

Like the Impressionists, Stravinsky's music is dependent upon sonorous "quantities," rather than upon the old devices of thematic development, repetition, harmonic sub-structure, and symmetrical balance of form. His methods of sonority-succession, correspondence, and contrast are based entirely upon objective investigation of their aural values, particularly with regard to their affinities—*i.e.,* the aural relationship or relativity of effect existing between any combination of sounds enunciated together, as compared with any other given combination of sounds. The ordinary academic classifications of chords are negated by him; he recognises in the term "chord" any combination of notes contributing to an individual sonority. With the Impressionists, however, such as Debussy, sound-quantities were utilised in a colourist manner, to suggest impressions—in a sense, therefore, to represent. With Stravinsky they are apprehended more concretely. Analogies are always dangerous; but, if one may compare the Impressionist methods to those of paint, Stravinsky, particularly in his later development, as manifest from "Le Sacre du Printemps" to the "Symphony for Wind-Instruments," dedicated to the memory of Debussy, approaches more closely those of sculpture. There is nothing in his work pertaining to the thin, surface-quality of accepted melodic theme-line; he treats his sonorities as complete wholes; the chord, if one may retain the term, is treated as an independent sound entity; its values are not those of intervals, but of mass, in which varied sounds create a kind of point-illism. Even where he presents melodic phrases, these are intrinsic to the general context of the rest of the music, not detached from the accompanying portions, as is the case with harmonised melody—*i.e.,* melody plus harmony. With Stravinsky thematic material and harmonic sub-texture cease to exist; his sonorities are one knit sound-substance, and he mingles them with others equally independent, on different aural planes, superimposed, and disposed according to the contrasts and correspondences justified by the pragmatic sanction of the aural sensation, the primary musical fact.

The orchestration of Stravinsky is equally objective. He differs from all preceding composers in that he treats his instruments, not as harmonic or contrapuntal accessories, but as intrinsic expressive media, investigating by direct experiment the individual *timbre* and characteristics of each, and seeking, by particularised treatment, to utilise their most extensive capacities, both independently and in combination with other instruments. All extraneous conventions are put aside. He negates the stiff grouping of the orchestra into "families" of wood-wind, brass, and strings; and he denies the old method of instrumental writing which was based on a conventional counterpoise and alternation of "masculine" and "feminine" feeling. The *timbre* of the instrument supplies a motive in the pattern, the phrase emphasising this; the note and *timbre* are regarded as of intrinsic unity. In a word, Stravinsky treats his orchestra *substantially*, not according to the old thesis of instrumentation. For him orchestration is the art of composing for instruments in unified design, in one fully conceived entity, as opposed to instrumentation—the tinting of themes conceived abstractly from this organic orchestral identity.

To the mobility of Stravinsky's music his keen analysis of the function of rhythm contributes greatly, revealing again the correspondence which his work bears to the impulses agitating the other arts, and invoking the attention of the world in more universal ways. In the rhythmic factor Stravinsky finds a unifying element which, far more efficiently than the ordinary formal or structural divisions of academic composition, creates for his music its strong sense of natural development and inevitability, and consequently striking individuality of character. Negating the detailed arithmetical implications of musical "time," he utilises the rhythmic movement of sound as a delineative factor, co-ordinating by its means all the constituent subtleties of musical decoration, sonority, and *timbre* of which his music is made up. From this treatment derives the immense centrifugal force which is one of the main characteristics of his work.

It is this concentration which, apart from all other spiritual or material considerations, and apart from the unique individuality of feeling and thought which it expresses, renders Stravinsky's work so typical of the contemporary spirit, so expressive of the universal impulse towards an empiric and pragmatic investigation of all phenomena, and a fresh evaluation, free from theoretical standards and conventional associations. It brings musical aesthetics into line with the type of thought by which alone can be achieved that reconstruction which is the sole salvation of the world from the ruin to the verge of which it has been brought by irrational ideals, false sentiments, and theoretical institutions which do not accord with the actualities of life.

# ECHOES OF BYRON

## By Thomas Moult

THE private lives of Lord Byron and Oscar Wilde have been the candle flames round which the moth-like in the world of art have danced away their immaturity. Since the 'nineties the Byron candle has seemed to burn dimly enough, but that is because its young partner had glittering reflections from the "artistic" life of the period; also, there was an unconscionable number of willing wings to be scorched. It is, indeed, by recalling the emotions stirred in men at the name of Wilde that we shall be able to appreciate the indescribable uproar caused by Mrs. Harriet Beecher-Stowe's exposure, half a century old, of the gravest among Byron's offences, that of his supposedly adulterous relations with his own half-sister. The difference is that in Byron's case the popular sympathy was for the artist, not against him. He had been the idol of a generation, and to see his image in the mud roused the public to fury and blinded it to all reason. The version which Mrs. Beecher-Stowe had given as a consequence of Lady Byron's direct confidences was generally rejected, and the original theory, that the poet had an impossible wife, has persisted to this day.

Side by side, the two flames still consume the air. At the semi-private publication, fifteen years back, of a curious book called *Astarte,* and written by a grandson of the poet, the Beecher-Stowe revelations were repeated, and the older of the candles has flared again, pathetically. Ralph Earl of Lovelace, the author of *Astarte*, was brought up by his grandmother, the poet's widow. The affection which coloured all his memories of Lady Byron doubtless did a good deal to engender the state of mind that gave birth to this attempt of his to vindicate her memory. It was a state of mind that took no heed of consequences; he was undeterred by the fact that the reputation of his famous grandfather would necessarily be dragged in an unpleasant way again before the public. The book gave sufficient reason, based not only on Lady Byron's own statement but on the actual letters of the half-sister concerned, why the separation of the poet and his wife should have occurred after only a single year of married life. With one or two notable exceptions (Henry James wrote a long letter of melancholy approval) the book was adversely received by

Lovelace's contemporaries, and his purpose misunderstood. The author died six months after its publication.

Lady Lovelace has written a memoir of her husband to vindicate him in his turn, and to explain the true motive behind the writing of *Astarte*. We gather from it that his passion was for truth at any cost. Born as he had been to a grievous heritage in the secret which was imparted to him as he grew towards manhood, this passion developed into an obsession. As with the obsessed mind always, he pursued his object ruthlessly, making the preparation of that single volume a life-task. It is useless to enquire of such a man, as a critic enquired at the publication, why he had set his hand to such unpleasantness. The answer would hardly have concerned itself with reasons. Nor would it now, on the republication of *Astarte* and the issue of Lady Lovelace's memoir.[4] The simple explanation is that a grave injustice was believed to have urgently needed redress. For that reason we do not need to withhold our admiration at the spirit which prompted Lord and Lady Lovelace to bring these volumes into being. The fact that a century has passed since that injustice was committed has, unfortunately, mattered not in the least, and they are the inevitable consequence of Mrs. Beecher-Stowe's unnecessary accusations. Unnecessary, because the vagaries of Lord Byron were his own affair, or the affair, at most, of those directly affected by them. Succeeding generations are not affected even indirectly, blood ties though there are certain to be.

Doubtless the two books are being eagerly acquired by the folk who never by any chance have read Byron's poetry or ever will. The serious reader, on the other hand, will bestir himself to echo the critic's question as to justification. The reconstruction of a great personality is always justification, of course; but the reconstructor must also have distinction. The multitude of Byron's biographers have lacked it; Byron himself, apart from his gift of poetry, was a very commonplace aristocrat... Or it often happens that a fellow artist is so impressed by the personality of a genius that his imagination re-creates that personality, though whether it proves to be a likeness or not matters nothing. Mr. Frank Harris's portrait of Oscar Wilde occurs to the mind as an example of this re-creation of personality; it will have an existence eventually quite

---

[4] *Ralph Earl of Lovelace: A Memoir.* By Mary Countess of Lovelace. *10s. 6d.* net. *Astarte: A Fragment of Truth Concerning George Lord Byron.* By Ralph Earl of Lovelace. *18s.* net. (Christophers.)

apart from the original. So does every great biography. In the case of *Astarte* there is no such purpose. It is simply an addition to the mass of writings on Byron's private actions which, bearing hardly ever on his art, have for well-nigh a hundred years given him a fictitious significance. There is no endeavour to satisfy the legitimate desire that some folk, usually artists themselves, might have to be acquainted with the poet's method of expression, the sources of his writing, the general atmosphere of his workshop. If we consider the really big figures among men, we know precious little of them beyond those things, nor would it be of account ultimately, except from the human standpoint, if we possessed further knowledge. By his works shall the artist be known, not by his family feuds. In the case of the moralist, the politician, the social reformer, private conduct may have a passing, relative importance, but, unlike theirs, an artist's influence is gained through the sinking of his personality in his work. His life, therefore, and the various aspects and manifestations of it, are no longer a matter of dates and deeds.

After all, can we not divine instinctively the whole private history of our artists, just as the Prince of Zémire's *savant* once divined it of mankind? M. Anatole France has compressed it for him into half a dozen words: they were born, they suffered, they died. If Lord Lovelace suffered, so did Lord Byron. In the same way as we know from Burns's poem written in dejection that he experienced remorse, we know it of Byron—

> "My days are in the yellow leaf:
> The flowers and fruits of love are gone:
> The worm, the canker, and the grief
> Are mine alone."

We know also, and it is of greater consequence, that he wrote "She Walks in Beauty" and "The Isles of Greece."